ALASKA
WildBerry
GUIDE & COOKBOOK

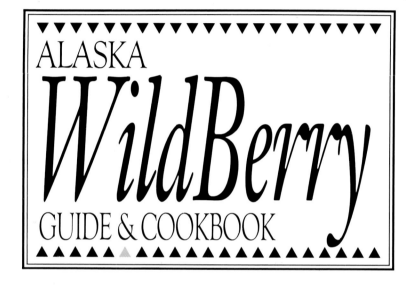

ALASKA
WildBerry
GUIDE & COOKBOOK

Alaska Northwest Books™

Anchorage • Seattle • Portland

First printing 1982
Ninth printing 2000

Library of Congress Cataloging-in-Publication Data
    Main entry under title:
    Berry book.
        Includes indexes.
        1. Cookery (Berries)   2. Berries—Alaska—
    Identification.   3. Wild plants, edible—Alaska—
    Identification.   I. Alaska magazine
    TX813.B4B46   1982   641.6'47   82-11393
    ISBN 0-88240-229-3

Illustrations by Virginia Howe
Design by Jon. Hersh
Cover design by Kate L. Thompson
Cover photograph by Lynn Hamrick

Alaska Northwest Books™
An imprint of Graphic Arts Center Publishing Company
P.O. Box 10306, Portland, OR 97296-0306
503-226-2402; www.gacpc.com

Printed in Singapore

CONTENTS

Foreword — vii

IDENTIFICATION GUIDE
— By Family —

CYPRESS — 2   *CROWFOOT — 10*   *GINSENG — 32*
LILY — 3   *SAXIFRAGE — 11*   *DOGWOOD — 33*
SANDALWOOD — 8   *ROSE — 17*   *HEATH — 36*
GOOSEFOOT — 9   *OLEASTER — 30*   *HONEYSUCKLE — 46*

RECIPES

BREADS — 55
  Biscuits and Buns — 56
  Muffins — 57
  Pancakes and Crepes — 59
  Specialty Breads — 61
  Coffee Cakes and Sweet Rolls — 64

SALADS AND DRESSINGS — 67

THE MAIN COURSE — 73
  Meat Dishes — 74
  Marinades — 78
  Stuffings — 79
  Dinner Sauces — 81
  Relishes — 85
  Catsups and Chutneys — 86

DESSERTS — 89
  Crusts — 90
  Pies, Tarts and Cobblers — 91
  Puddings, Steamed Puddings and
    Tapiocas — 103
  Cakes, Cupcakes, Tortes and
    Frostings — 110
  Shortcakes — 122
  Cookies and Bars — 124
  Frozen or Chilled Desserts — 129
  Mincemeats — 135
  Dessert Sauces — 136

BEVERAGES — 141
  Juices — 142
  Milk Shakes — 142
  Punches Without Alcohol — 143
  Punches With Alcohol — 145
  Wines, Liqueurs and Meads — 146

POTPOURRI — 151
  Candies — 152
  Syrups — 154
  Trail Foods — 157
  Eskimo and Indian Dishes — 158

PRESERVES — 159
  Jellies — 160
  Jams, Marmalades, Conserves
    and Butters — 165

CANNING BERRIES — 169

FREEZING BERRIES — 175

DRYING BERRIES — 181

GLOSSARY — 185

INDEXES

Index by Family Names — 188   *Index by Common Names — 192*
Index by Botanical Names — 190   *Recipe Index — 195*

FOREWORD

Nature provides us with no more delicious, nourishing or prolific food than the berries that grow in wild abandon throughout our Northern landscape. Indians and Eskimos have been aware of their value for centuries. The rest of us will, if we happen upon a raspberry patch, pick a luscious handful to munch along our way, or we may spend an hour or two collecting a bucketful of blueberries for the traditional pie. But we have been slower than the indigenous peoples in recognizing their basic worth. Now, with constantly rising cost of food, we are beginning to take up the slack with our wild fruit; we can emulate the Indians and Eskimos to our advantage.

We have tried here to provide a book that will be equally useful to the outdoorsman and the housewife. Nearly 50 species of berries that grow wild in Alaska are presented with accurate descriptions backed up by full-color photographs and black-and-white drawings. With this book in hand, anyone should be able to make the correct identifications in the field with confidence.

Most of these berries are edible, many a real treat to the taste buds. **Be sure to avoid the species shown as "poisonous" and those that are labeled "inedible."** There are plenty of berries that are a delight to eat and the questionable ones are not needed.

Much of our vast state has not been prospected for berry patches and may never be by any creature except the bears. Beware of them! Berries are an important food resource for bears, but they are not vegetarians. Not only should you leave a bear undisturbed if you find one at work in the patch you were planning to harvest, it is not considered good manners to intrude on other humans who may have arrived before you. Go find another patch. There are plenty around.

Berry picking is a wonderful family project — and so is eating the proceeds. This book presents a choice selection of 277 recipes that range far beyond the usual limited sampling of pies, toppings and jams. Besides desserts, you'll find, among other categories, recipes for beverages, marinades and meat dishes, stuffings, candies, sauces, trail foods and even wines. Also included is invaluable information on a multitude of ways to preserve berries. And if you live in a city and don't like to leave it, even for an hour, or if berry picking isn't your thing, cultivated varieties can be substituted for most of the wild berries in the recipes.

Alaska Wild Berry Trails, a book no longer in print, was a valuable resource for developing recipes.

The primary source we have consulted for identification of our wild fruits has been *Flora of Alaska and Neighboring Territories,* an authoritative work by the eminent Swedish botanist, Eric Hulten. In the main, most other authors agree with his classifications, although there always seems to be some disagreement among botanical authors regarding identifications. Other references of value are the U.S. government publication, Agriculture Handbook No. 410, *Alaska Trees and Shrubs,* by Leslie A. Viereck and Elbert L. Little, Jr. Two bulletins produced by the University of Alaska Cooperative Extension Service, *Wild Edible and Poisonous Plants of Alaska* and *Wild Berry Recipes* are also useful.

We wish to give grateful acknowledgment to Aline Strutz for her invaluable assistance in the preparation of the identification section and to Dr. Stanley L. Welsh for his review of photographic material. Any errors that may remain are ours alone. We also wish to thank Virginia Howie for preparing the botanical drawings of the various species. Finally, we offer special thanks to the many contributors of photographs and recipes that comprise this book.

—The Editors

HEATH FAMILY

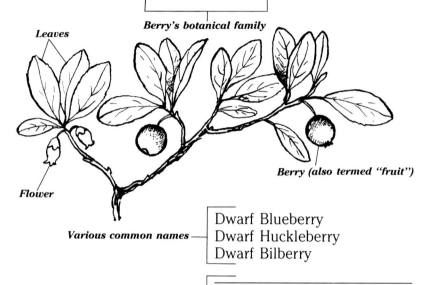

Leaves

Berry's botanical family

Flower

Berry (also termed "fruit")

Various common names ─
Dwarf Blueberry
Dwarf Huckleberry
Dwarf Bilberry

Botanical name by genus and species ─
Vaccinium caespitosum

Low shrub with shiny green leaves, variable in form but always toothed. To 14 inches; often matted; urn-shaped flowers borne singly at base of leaf clusters. Berries with a whitish "bloom" (a powdery coating over the surface of berries or leaves of certain species). Common in bogs, mountain meadows and open, coastal forests from south slopes of Alaska Range to Prince William Sound and south through Southeastern Alaska to northern California and east to the northern Rockies; eastern Canada and New England. Sweet fruit ripens in August.

Further information about each berry's form, habitat, and range as well as comments about usefulness and edibility.

Identification Guide

Alaska Berries and Their Names

In some parts of the North wild berries have different common names, and this is why we need botanical names too. For example, the berry we know in the Anchorage area as "crowberry" is called "blackberry" by many western Alaskans. They are indeed black but certainly nothing like the blackberries of Washington and Oregon. Another crowberry alias is "mossberry." Whatever the common names used, the botanical name for this plant is *Empetrum nigrum* anywhere in the world.

The salmonberry of Western Alaska is "cloudberry" or "baked apple berry" in southcentral Alaska. It is *Rubus chamaemorus*. Incidentally, this plant ranges over most of Alaska. In the coastal regions of Alaska from the mid-Aleutians to Southeastern Alaska there is a tall shrub which has either red or salmon-colored fruit. It is called "salmonberry" in this area. The botanical name is *Rubus spectabilis*. Both salmonberries are delicious. Don't be surprised, then, at other names given to our berries that do not agree with names you know them by.

Perhaps the lowbush cranberry or lingonberry is more useful than any other Northern wild berry. Maybe it just seems so because it is so prevalent in Canada and Alaska. In fact, it is at home over a great part of the Northern Hemisphere. One form or another of the popular blueberry is circumboreal, too. The type of blueberry that grows at the higher altitudes seems to be sweeter, as you may have noticed; larger, also. Wild roses are native to much of the North Country and so are red raspberries. One variety of our sweet wild strawberries grows along the coast clear to Chile. Wild strawberries are not often found in abundance but there is no better wild fruit.

Juniper
Common Juniper
Mountain Juniper

Juniperus communis

Low shrub with sprawling habit, needlelike foliage and berrylike small cones that are green the first year. They ripen the second year and usually are covered with a bluish bloom. Dry places, particularly in subalpine locations. In much of Alaska except for Western Alaska and the North Slope (a few in the Colville River Basin); circumboreal and in scattered habitats elsewhere. Edible; sometimes used as a seasoning for meat dishes.

Dick L. Byrd

Blue Bead
Single-Flowered Clintonia
Queen's Cup

Clintonia uniflora

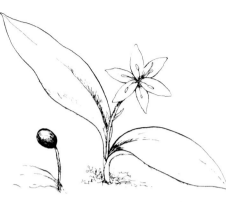

Smilacina borealis of some authors. Small plant with a few large, clasping leaves. To 8 inches. White or creamy solitary flowers. The fruit resembles a large, blue bead. Shady woods and clearings. From Southeastern Alaska to California and east to the northern Rocky Mountains. Not considered edible.

Maxcine Williams

William D. Boehm

False Solomon's Seal
Star-Flowered Solomon's Seal

Smilacina stellata

Plant with large, pointed, clasping, alternate leaves. To 16 inches. Tiny, creamy flowers borne in a raceme. Mottled berries ripen to red or reddish black in August. Wet meadows and tidal flats. Found sparingly in Alaska, specifically at Eklutna Flats near Anchorage; southern Yukon Territory and southward through California; east through southern Canada and the United States, exclusive of the southern tier of states. Not considered edible.

S. racemosa is a similar plant found in extreme Southeastern Alaska, southward through Oregon; in the Rocky Mountain zone and east to the Atlantic seaboard.

Zolton Gaal, Jr.

R.W. Tyler

Deerberry
False Lily-of-the-Valley
Wild Lily-of-the-Valley

Maianthemum dilatatum

Unifolium dilatatum of some authors. Small plant with one or two large, heart-shaped leaves and a raceme of creamy white flowers extending above the leaves. To 14 inches. Ripens into red berries. Woods, thickets and tundra. Coastal from Prince William Sound to California and east to the northwestern Rocky Mountains; westernmost Aleutian Islands and eastern Asia, including Japan. Not considered edible.

Richard H. Norton

Richard H. Norton

Twisted Stalk
Watermelon Berry
Cucumber Root

Streptopus amplexifolius

Large, clasping leaves on forked branches shelter a short, twisted or kinky flower stem. To 4 feet. The whole plant has a cucumberlike odor. Creamy white flowers ripen into extremely juicy, red, melon-shaped berries, about ½ inch long, in August. Moist woods, meadows and thickets. From Yukon River Valley to northern California and Mexico; northeastern Canada and United States; scattered locales in Asia and Europe. Edible, although seldom found in large enough quantities to use alone. Tender shoots can be eaten raw in salads; berries can be combined with others or used in syrups.

Ernest Manewal

Alice Puster

Rosy Twisted Stalk

Streptopus roseus

Flower stemlets not actually twisted as in *S. amplexifolius.* Single, unbranched stalk with large, clasping leaves and rosy pink flowers almost hidden by foliage. To 4 feet. The juicy, red berry ripens in late summer. Thickets and forests in southeastern portion of Alaska, south to Washington; also in northeastern part of North America. Edible.

Ernest Manewal

Maxcine Williams

Northern Commandra
Timberberry

Geocaulon lividum

Inconspicuous plant of open forest floor. To 8 inches. Orange-red berry ripens in late summer. Leaves, light green at flowering stage, may or may not turn rusty, burgundy red as berries ripen depending on the individual specimen and locality. From upper Cook Inlet throughout the Interior, south and east into Yukon Territory, northern British Columbia and across Canada to the Eastern Seaboard. Edible, but rarely collected.

Kenneth Roberson

Mary V. Smith

Strawberry Blite
Strawberry Spinach
Squaw Paint

Chenopodium capitatum

Sprawling annual plant with weak stems and light green leaves shaped like a goose track. To 2 feet. The strawberrylike fruit grows close to the stem and clear to the top. River bars and other waste places. Interior and Southcentral Alaska, east and south through the Rocky Mountain States and to eastern Canada and Massachusetts. Not considered edible. The fruiting stems are lovely in flower arrangements.

Lu Liston, reprinted from *The Alaska-Yukon Wild Flowers Guide*

Barbara D. Kalen

Baneberry

Actaea rubra

Deadly POISONOUS. Under no circumstances should these berries be collected. Stout plant. To 4 feet. Racemes of tiny, whitish flowers spring from the upright plant with compound, toothed leaves. Berries are between ¼ and ½ inch long and ripen to scarlet or white. The white berries are sometimes called "doll's eyes" because of their black tips resembling the pupil of a doll's eye. Open woods and dry hillsides. Coastal Alaska through the southeastern portion; north beyond the Alaska Range to the Yukon River Valley and east through northern North America.

Elfrida Nord

Dorothy T. Simpson

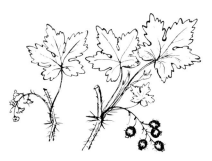

Bristly Black Currant
Swamp Gooseberry

Ribes lacustre

Like many currants, this one has an unpleasant odor. Sharp spines clothe the twigs of the erect to sprawling shrub. To 4 feet. Flowers occur in drooping racemes, followed by purplish or blackish fruit normally ripening in August. Moist woods and woods near streams. Alaska Peninsula northeast to the foothills of the Alaska Range; north of the Alaska Range, east and southeast through Canada to the northeastern coast of North America; northern Japan. Considered edible, but not particularly appetizing.

Janet Klein

Barbara D. Kalen

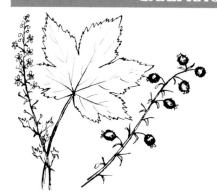

Stink Currant

Ribes bracteosum

A malodorous shrub with spreading or erect habit. To 7 feet. The white flowers occur in upright racemes and in late July or early August give way to black berries. Woods and stream sides. From Kenai Peninsula along the coast to northern California. Edible, but unsavory and not recommended.

Mari Hurley

Maxcine Williams

Northern Black Currant

Ribes hudsonianum

An ascending shrub with white flowers borne on racemes. To 6 feet. Bitter black fruit usually ripens in August. Moist woods and stream sides. Alaska Peninsula north and east to the Brooks Range foothills and east through Canada and the northern United States to the Great Lakes region. Edible, but not recommended.

Aline Strutz

Dorothy T. Simpson

Skunk Currant

Ribes glandulosum

Erect shrub with unpleasant odor. To 3 feet. Flowers are white to pinkish, drooping as the heavier red fruit ripens in July or August. Berries are clothed with bristles. Woods or stony slopes. Alaska Peninsula north and east to the Yukon River Valley and east through Canada and New England. Edible, but not recommended.

Dick L. Byrd

Trailing Black Currant

Ribes laxiflorum

Trailing, spreading branches to 8 feet long. Flowers borne in racemes are greenish white or reddish, and the fruit, which ripens in August, is black. Moist woods and roadsides. Kenai Peninsula north to Alaska Range foothills and south to foothills of the Rocky Mountains and into northern California. Birds are fond of the fruit and often strip the branches. Its leaves are among the first to turn scarlet. Edible, but not choice.

Rose Arvidson

Jerry Taylor

Northern Red Currant
American Red Currant

Ribes triste

Spreading shrub. To 4 feet. With purplish or pinkish flowers on racemes, drooping as the shiny, red, translucent currants ripen in August. From the lower meadows to timber line, particularly along streams and in thickets. Ranges from the Chukchi Peninsula in Siberia through most of Alaska except the Arctic, Aleutian Islands and southern part of the Panhandle; Canada and northwestern United States. Probably the most sought after of all our wild currants, it makes delicious jam and jelly.

Jim Shives

Charles Kay

Kenneth Roberson

Oregon Crab Apple
Western Crab Apple

Malus fusca

A small tree or shrub. To 15 feet. Apple blossoms are typically white or pink. Bears small, purplish fruit, longer than broad, that mature in September and October. Open woods. Kenai Peninsula (sparingly) and Southeastern Alaska; south along the coast to central California. Edible, but seldom found in enough quantity for use.

Mari Hurley

Sitka Mountain Ash

Sorbus sitchensis

Shrub with reddish bark. To 8 feet. Its white flowers develop into red or orange-red berries, often with a bluish bloom. Ripens in August and September. In woods from low to subalpine areas. From Alaska Peninsula, Kodiak Island, Kenai Peninsula and coastal regions to northern California. Not considered edible.

S. scopulina is another shrubby mountain ash that grows slightly taller than Sitka mountain ash and has compound, toothed leaves. Its fruit is orange to red and glossy, and it is found in much the same areas. Edible.

Ernest Manewal

Janet Klein

Serviceberry
Shadbush
Juneberry
Pacific Serviceberry

Amelanchier alnifolia

Said to bloom when the shad are running in some areas of the country. Usually a low shrub on wind-swept hillsides, sometimes reaching 15 feet in the southern part of the range. Flowers are white in a rounded raceme and leaves are toothed. Berries are almost black with a purplish bloom. Moist woods and hillsides. Kenai Peninsula, Chugach foothills, Yukon River Valley south and east through Yukon Territory and Northwest Territories, British Columbia, Washington and Oregon; east to Ontario and Minnesota. Edible, but rather insipid; better cooked.

   A. florida (Pacific serviceberry) is a taller shrub which grows in forest clearings and damp woods. Insipid, but edible.

Jon R. Nickles

Maxcine Williams

Five-Leaved Bramble
Trailing Raspberry

Rubus pedatus

Creeping or trailing small plant with leaves made up of 5 leaflets. White flowers are followed in late July by small, juicy, red raspberrylike fruits about ¼ the size of the average raspberry. Damp forest floor and mossy areas. Coastal along Alaska Peninsula, Kodiak Island and Alaska Range; east to the Rocky Mountain foothills and southward to central California. Edible.

M. Hudson

Maxcine Williams

Cloudberry
Baked Apple Berry
Salmonberry

Rubus chamaemorus

Many Western Alaskans prefer the name of salmonberry for this fruit because of its color. Small, upright plant with comparatively large leaves. To 8 inches. It bears a single white flower. Juicy, raspberrylike fruit ripens in August. Peat bogs and tundra. Most of Alaska except for mid-Aleutian Islands; circumboreal. Edible.

Jon R. Nickles

David F. Hatler

Nagoonberry
Wineberry

Rubus arcticus
(Rubus stellatus)

Small plant with rosy red flowers borne among dainty leaves subdivided into threes. To 5 inches. Fruit is small, raspberrylike and red to reddish purple. Shady thickets, meadows and stream sides. Most of Alaska except northwestern part, Aleutian Islands, the western Alaska Peninsula and the Cook Inlet area south to Southeastern Alaska; range extends eastward and southward to the Rocky Mountains; almost circumboreal. Edible.

Jon R. Nickles

Gary Dobos

Raspberry
Red Raspberry

Rubus idaeus

Woody, prickly shrub. To 6 feet. Bears white flowers with typical red raspberry fruits in late July and August. Inhabits thickets and forest edges; often near water or along roadsides in full sun, where they tend to be shorter and the fruit smaller. Across central Alaska, eastern Alaska Peninsula and Kodiak Island; east and south through Canada and the United States to the eastern seaboard; south through Washington to northern Mexico. Edible.

Richard Rife

Maxcine Williams

Salmonberry

Rubus spectabilis

Biennial woody shrub. To 7 feet. Often occurs with prickles on the twigs. Leaves are made up of three toothed leaflets. Rosy purple flowers are followed in late summer by salmon-yellow or red fruit, similar in appearance to large raspberries. Often forms tangled thickets in moist woods or on subalpine slopes. Aleutian Islands, Kodiak Island and coastal to California. Edible.

John J. Koranda

Andrew Gronholdt

Ernest Manewal

Wild Strawberry
Fragaria virginiana

Typical small strawberry plant. To 6 inches. Bears white flowers, scarlet fruit and seeds sunk in pits. Open woods and hillsides. From midway in the Yukon River Valley east and south through southern Yukon Territory to the eastern seaboard and as far south as California and Georgia. Edible.

Aline Strutz

Paul R. Clark

Mary Clay Muller

Thimbleberry
Rubus parviflorus

Shrub with erect, brownish branches and no prickles; large, maplelike leaves. To 6 feet. Flowers are white with soft, juicy, pale red fruit ripening in August and sometimes as late as September. Blossoms, green fruit and ripe fruit occasionally may be seen on the plants at one time. Forest openings, along streams and in thickets. Southeastern Alaska and south in mountainous areas to California and the Rockies; east as far as Ontario, Minnesota and the Great Lakes region. Edible, but it takes a great many to fill a pail.

Barbara D. Kalen

Barbara D. Kalen

Beach Strawberry
Fragaria chiloensis

Plant with sprawling habit. To 6 inches. Flowers are white, and its scarlet fruit ripens in July and August. Similar in appearance to a small, cultivated strawberry. Coastal from Aleutian Islands and Kodiak Island (excluding most of the Alaska Peninsula) to southern California; also coastal in South America. Edible. Both *F. chiloensis* and *F. virginiana* (wild strawberry) are prized for jam.

Rose Arvidson

Black Raspberry
Black Cap

Rubus leucodermis

Woody shrub with prickly, whitish
bark. To 6 feet. White flower clusters
are followed by blackish raspberries.
Forest edges, thickets and clearings.
Southeastern Alaska south through
British Columbia to California and
northern Rocky Mountain states. Rarely
found in Alaska. Edible.

Bruce H. Barritt

Kenneth Roberson

Prickly Wild Rose
Wild Rose
Nootka Rose
Woods Rose

Rosa acicularis

A shrubby plant. To 6 feet. Large, rosy flowers are borne singly on prickly twigs. The orange-red fruit (rose hip) matures in August and September and is usually best when picked after the first frost. Bogs, woods, and clearings. From Colville River and southern slopes of the Brooks Range covering most of Alaska except the Aleutian Islands, Alaska Peninsula, North Slope and Southeastern Alaska. Almost circumboreal. Rose hips are edible, rich in vitamin C and are used extensively in syrups, jams and other delicacies. Other rose hip-bearing species: *R. nutkana* (Nootka rose), found on Kodiak Island, the Cook Inlet area and Southeastern Alaska; and *R. woodsii* (woods rose), inhabiting certain small areas of Interior Alaska, western Canada and down into the Rocky Mountains.

Richard Rife

Paul R. Clark

Charles Kay

Soapberry
Soopalallie

Shepherdia canadensis

A scurfy appearing, sprawling shrub. To 6 feet. With male and female flowers, yellowish or brown, borne on different plants in May. Orange-red fruits ripen in July. Forest, gravel bars and dry slopes. Most of the state except the northeastern portion, Western and lower Southeastern Alaska; across the continent to northeastern Canada. Edible, but bitter. When beaten it forms a frothy mass like soapsuds.

Dorothy T. Simpson

Silverberry

Elaeagnus commutata

A shrub with an overall sheen of silvery green. To 10 feet. The small, fragrant flowers are pale yellow. Comparatively large, silvery berries mature in August. Dry slopes, sandy or gravelly banks of rivers and river bars. Scattered stations in the Interior, Matanuska Valley, Yukon Territory and British Columbia; more widespread in southern Canada, eastern Washington and the northern Rocky Mountain states. Said to be edible, but are dry and mealy and certainly not appealing.

Maxcine Williams

Maxcine Williams

Devil's Club

Echinopanax horridum (Oplopanax horridum)

Coarse, woody, deciduous shrub. To 10 feet. Armed with wicked yellow spines and has large, maplelike, shiny leaves. Flowers are small, creamy white, crowded on upright stalk. Fruit is vivid scarlet. Damp habitats on hillsides and in woods. Kodiak Island north and east through the Matanuska and Susitna valleys; more or less coastal to northern California. Not considered edible.

Zoltan Gaal, Jr.

Gary Dobos

Red-Osier Dogwood
American Dogwood
Red Stem Dogwood

Cornus stolonifera

Woody shrub with red bark. To 12 feet. White flowers grow in clusters in June and July. The whitish fruit matures in August and September. Open woods, along streams and edges of clearings. From Yukon River Valley south and east through southern Yukon Territory and the Rocky Mountains to Mexico; across the continent to northeastern United States. Not considered edible, but useful as an ornamental plant and easily grown. Beautiful in autumn.

Aline Strutz

Charles Kay

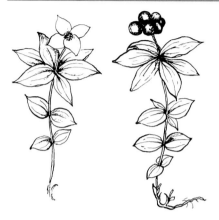

Swedish Cornel
Lapland Cornel

Cornus suecica

Similar to *C. canadensis* (bunchberry) but with several extra sets of leaves arranged in whorls around the stem. To 8 inches. The minute white flowers give way to rosy red berries in August and September. Open woods, marshes and bogs, and subalpine habitats. Eastern Siberia through Western Alaska, including Aleutian Islands and along the coast through British Columbia and northern Washington; northeastern Canada, Greenland and Europe. Edible, but insipid. The bunchberry and the Swedish cornel often hybridize where their ranges overlap.

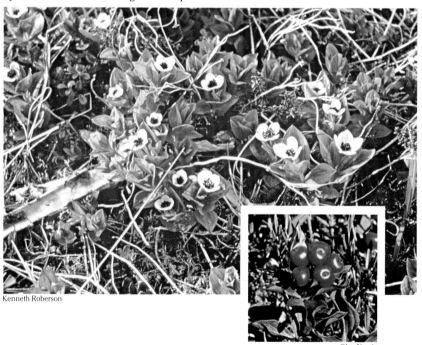

Kenneth Roberson

Olga Norris

Bunchberry
Canadian Dwarf Dogwood
Dwarf Cornel
Miniature Dogwood

Cornus canadensis

To 8 inches. Four white, petallike bracts surround a cluster of tiny flowers (the whole appearing like one larger flower) which develop into bright red berries in a cluster or bunch. Berries ripen in August and September.

Birch and spruce forests up to subalpine habitats. Most of the state, Yukon Territory, south and east to central California, New England and Virginia. Edible, but insipid and dry and better used in combination with other fruit.

William D. Boehm

Third Eye Photography

Crowberry
Mossberry
Black Berry

Empetrum nigrum

A creeping plant, similar to some heathers in appearance. Evergreen, needlelike foliage with inconspicuous flowers. The berry is small, shiny and black, ripening in August and often persisting through the winter. Tundra, bogs, muskegs, mountain slopes, forest edges. Widespread in Alaska, appearing everywhere except in the High Arctic; east and south through Canada and northern United States; circumboreal. Edible, but insipid and better when cooked; best used in combination with other berries.

Sundog Photography

Maxcine Williams

Salal

Gaultheria shallon

Erect or sprawling evergreen shrub. To 4 feet. Flowers are small, pinkish bells with fleshy, blackish purple fruit ripening in July and August. An undershrub in woods in lower portion of Southeastern Alaska and through northern California. Edible, but seldom collected for food. Florists designate the branches as "lemon leaves."

Another species of *Gaultheria, G. miqueliana,* is found in Alaska only on Kiska Island in the Aleutians, and in Japan.

Victor B. Scheffer   Inset: Maxcine Williams

Kinnikinnick
Bearberry
Meal Berry

Arctostaphylos uva-ursi

Creeping, mat-forming evergreen shrub with long, trailing branches. Flowers are white or pinkish, urn-shaped bells. Small, mealy red berries ripen in August to September. Sandy or gravelly places along roadsides, open woods or other dry places. Most of Alaska except for the western reaches and the lower portion of Southeastern Alaska; almost circumboreal. The insipid berries are better cooked than raw, but not especially flavorful in either case. It's been reported that the dried leaves once were crumbled and used as a substitute for tobacco.

Aline Strutz

Bearberry
Alpine Bearberry
Ptarmigan Berry

Arctostaphylos alpina

Trailing, mat-forming dwarf shrub with white flowers and black fruit maturing in August. Arctic and alpine tundra, mountain slopes, woods. Another species, *A. rubra*, is similar except that its leaves are larger, its fruit are scarlet berries, and it is generally found in lower altitudes. Together, the two cover most of Alaska except for the Aleutian Islands and the lower portion of Southeastern Alaska; almost circumboreal. Both species are capable of turning large expanses of their native habitat into sheets of scarlet as their foliage changes color in autumn. Edible; bears are said to be fond of these, but the berries are rather tasteless.

Tom Falley

Kenneth Roberson

Lowbush Cranberry
Lingonberry
Mountain Cranberry

Vaccinium vitis-idaea

A creeping evergreen shrub. Flowers are small, pink bells, and fruit is deep red when ripe in August and September. Woods, thickets, mountain slopes and tundra. All of Alaska including the offshore islands; circumboreal. Edible; probably the most useful of all Alaska's berries; best collected just after the first frost. The acidic fruit often persists through the winter.

Alice Puster

Zolton Gaal, Jr.

Red Huckleberry
Vaccinium parvifolium

A shrub with light green foliage. To 10 feet. Greenish white, yellow or pink, urn-shaped flowers. Berries are bright red, ripening in August. An undershrub in forests. Endemic from Yakutat southward along the coast to northern California. Sour, but edible and choice.

Victor B. Scheffer

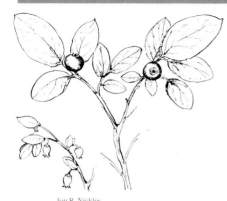

Jon R. Nickles

Early Blueberry
Blue Huckleberry

Vaccinium ovalifolium

This earliest of our blueberries is a sprawling shrub, often with a reddish stem. To 5 feet. Flowers are pink and urn-shaped. Fruit ripens to a dark bluish purple with a whitish bloom in mid-July through August. Clearings, open woods and thickets. Kodiak Island and Talkeetna Mountains; coastal and southward through Southeastern Alaska to northern California. Scattered other habitats in North America. Edible.

Aline Strutz

Alaska Blueberry
Vaccinium alaskensis

V. alaskaense of some authors. Similar to *V. ovalifolium* but taller and with larger leaves. To 6½ feet. Pink, urn-shaped flowers are followed in late July and August by blue-black berries. Often an understory shrub of spruce and hemlock forests; forest clearings. Endemic from Kenai Peninsula through Southeastern Alaska, British Columbia and Washington. Edible.

Jerry Taylor

Jerry Taylor

Bog Blueberry
Alpine Blueberry
Bog Bilberry
Whortleberry

Vaccinium uliginosum

Strongly branched, low shrub with typical blueberry blossoms. To 12 inches. Fruit ripens in August and is blue or almost black with a bluish bloom. Bogs and open lands. Most widely spread of Alaskan blueberries, found everywhere except the offshore islands and the extreme Arctic; circumboreal. Edible.

Jerry Taylor

Third Eye Photography

Bog Cranberry
True Cranberry
Swamp Cranberry

Oxycoccus microcarpus

Prostrate, creeping shrub with slender branches and tiny leaves. Sometimes the whole plant seems to be buried in moss except for the flowers, and the berries appear to lie like rubies on green velvet. The flowers resemble miniature shooting stars. Mossy peat bogs. Most of Alaska except for the North Slope and westernmost Aleutian Islands; one station has been found in Colville River Valley in the Arctic; almost circumpolar. Seldom abundant enough for collecting in any quantity. Edible.

Dorothy T. Simpson

Rose Arvidson

Red Elderberry
Pacific Red Elder

Sambucus racemosa

Seeds of this species are said to be POISONOUS. It is probably best left alone. Tall shrub with pithy stems. To 12 feet. The small, creamy-white flower clusters have an unpleasant scent. Small, red berries follow the flowers in July and August at the same time *Echinopanax horridum* (devil's club) is bearing its red blossoms, and they are often found growing in close proximity. Woods and subalpine meadows, roadsides and hillsides in the shade. Coastal from Alaska Peninsula to California; southwestern and northwestern Canada, and the United States; almost circumboreal.

June Mackie

Jim Shives

Jon R. Nickles

Highbush Cranberry
Viburnum edule

Erect shrub, sometimes straggly. To 10 feet but usually shorter. Coarsely toothed leaves are shaped similar to maple leaves. Small, creamy flowers in a cluster develop into ripe red fruit in August and September. Clearings, forest edges, thickets and subalpine slopes or beside water. Alaska Peninsula north to the Brooks Range; throughout Canada; east and south to Pennsylvania and Oregon. Edible, but best gathered before completely ripe.

Len Sherwin

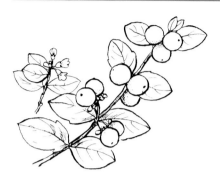

Snowberry
Symphoricarpus albus

An erect shrub. To 4½ feet. Grows pinkish or whitish flowers. White "snow" berries mature in August or September. Woods, thickets and roadsides. Has a limited range in the state, found only in the upper part of Southeastern Alaska; extends southward from British Columbia to the Rocky Mountains and California. A similar species grows across Canada from eastern British Columbia and in the northern part of the United States. Not considered edible, but suitable for ornamental plantings.

Bob Hagel

Ernest Manewal

Honeysuckle
Black Twinberry
Bearberry Honeysuckle

Lonicera involucrata

Reported to be POISONOUS. It is probably best left alone. A sprawling shrub. To 10 feet. Yellow flowers, which sometimes appear with a purplish tinge, are borne in pairs. The twin berries are black and ripen in late summer. Moist woods and forest edge. Rare in Alaska; found only in Southeastern Alaska (sparingly); British Columbia across the continent to Quebec; south to California and the Rocky Mountain states to Mexico.

Maxcine Williams

Maxcine Williams

Gary Dobos

A patch of Alpine bearberry
(Arctostaphylos alpina) spreads a
scarlet sheet over the ground in Denali
National Park and Preserve. Both
A. alpina and a similar species, *A. rubra,*
occur throughout Alaska, excluding the
Aleutian Islands and the lower portion of
Southeastern Alaska, turning the
countryside red in autumn.

Recipes

A Little About Berries as Food

In this volume we have concentrated our recipes among the more abundant or more popular species of wild berries. Many berries native to other regions are similar to ours and can be used in place of the Northern fruit suggested for recipes here. Cultivated species may also be substituted for wild berries, although one must remember that they are often less tart than their wild relatives and adjustments in the sugar added may be necessary.

The different forms of raspberries may be substituted one for the other and blueberries likewise. The red currant is a distinctive fruit, and it is probably best not to use other varieties of currants when a recipe calls for red ones. Lowbush and highbush cranberries are entirely different and require different recipes.

The farther north one can collect rose hips (fruit of the rose), the more Vitamin C content they will have. They are extremely useful in the North where Vitamin C is so lacking and oranges so expensive! They can be used alone or with other fruit. Rose hips should definitely be harvested whenever available. There is difference of opinion about when to harvest. Some people say they should be picked just before the first frost and others prefer to pluck them after the frost.

Wild crab apples are not berries but they are included in this book because they are our only Northern tree fruit. They are often little more than shrubs but are well worth gathering when found in enough abundance.

Many of the recipes given here are in the dessert category, but you may be surprised by how many other ways there are to use wild berries. Lowbush cranberries are particularly good in certain meat dishes and are useful as a marinade for meat. Wild berries are fine for jam and jelly making, of course, not to mention for drying and freezing.

Food preparation often involves a certain amount of experimentation, so do try new combinations and methods and be an experimenter yourself. You may have some delightful eating if you are brave enough to venture changes in recipes. At any rate wild berries are fun to work with from the time of harvest through the eating. We think you will agree.

BREADS

Blueberry Pan Biscuits

1 cup blueberries (huckleberries
  are good, too)
2 cups flour
2 teaspoons baking powder

1 teaspoon salt
2 tablespoons vegetable oil
2/3 cup milk

Grease and preheat on top of stove a large cast-iron skillet (don't let it get smoking hot). Mix berries and dry ingredients together in bowl. Add oil and mix together and stir until dough is soft. Do not beat. Drop by spoonfuls onto the heated skillet. Cover with lid and place on low heat, cooking dough about 10 minutes on each side. Serve hot with butter and honey.

Variation: Try Berry Drop Biscuits, using the same ingredients (or a biscuit mix). Add 3 tablespoons brown sugar. Drop from a spoon onto a cookie sheet or large cast-iron skillet and bake from 15 to 20 minutes in a 400° oven.

Karen Jettmar
Gustavus, Alaska

Stuffed Biscuits

Biscuit mix
1 cup walnuts
1/4 cup candied orange peel
1 tablespoon dried orange peel
  (or bits)

1/2 cup Whole Berry Cranberry
  Sauce (see recipe, page 84)
1/2 cup creamed butter
  or margarine
Honey
Strawberry jam

Bake biscuits according to package directions. For the stuffing mixture: chop the nuts fine and mix with the candied and dried orange peel and berry sauce; blend in butter, a little at a time, and moisten further with enough honey to make it spreadable. Split the baked biscuits and stuff with berry mixture. Allow to cool. Wrap biscuits in foil and freeze. To be their best, these stuffed biscuits should be made up at least 10 days before needed. To serve: preheat oven to 400°; place foil-wrapped biscuits on a cookie sheet and bake for 6 to 8 minutes; unwrap and bake for another 2 minutes. Strawberry jam with nuts makes a fine stuffing for biscuits, too.

Jam Buns

2 cups flour
3 teaspoons baking powder
2 tablespoons sugar
1/4 teaspoon salt
1 cup shortening

1 slightly beaten egg
1/2 cup milk
1 teaspoon vanilla
Wild berry jam

Sift together flour, baking powder, sugar and salt. Cream shortening and egg together, then gradually add the milk and vanilla. Slowly mix in the dry ingredients. Roll out the dough on a lightly floured board and cut into 3-inch squares. Drop a spoonful of any wild berry jam onto the center of half the squares. Cover with remaining squares. Pinch edges together to seal and place in oiled muffin pans. Bake in oven at 375° for 15 minutes or until well browned. These are goodies for after school.

MUFFINS

Berry Wheat Muffins

1/2 to 3/4 cup *dried* wild berries
1/2 cup toasted wheat germ
1 cup stone-ground, wholewheat
   flour
1/2 cup all-purpose flour
1/2 teaspoon salt

1-1/2 teaspoons baking soda
1/2 cup sugar
8 ounces plain yogurt
2 eggs
1/4 cup corn oil

Preheat oven to 400°. Combine berries and dry ingredients. Mix the yogurt, eggs and oil together and pour over the dry ingredients. Stir just enough to moisten but do not beat. Spoon batter into paper-lined muffin cups, filling each about 3/4 full. Bake for 18 to 20 minutes or until the muffins test as done. Serve with lots of butter while they're still warm.

Blueberry Muffins

1/4 cup butter
2 slightly beaten eggs
1/2 teaspoon salt
1 cup sugar
2 cups flour

2 teaspoons baking powder
1/2 cup milk
1 teaspoon vanilla
2 cups fresh, frozen or canned
   (drained) blueberries

In mixing bowl beat together butter, eggs, salt and sugar. Sift flour and baking powder together and add, alternately, with the milk to the first mixture. Stir in the vanilla. Add the blueberries. Bake in muffin pans at 350° for 25 minutes.

Pacific Northwest
Blueberry Growers Association

Lowbush Cranberry Muffins

3/4 cup lowbush cranberries
3/4 cup powdered sugar
2 cups flour
3 teaspoons baking powder
1 scant teaspoon salt

1/4 cup granulated sugar
1 cup milk
1 well-beaten egg
4 tablespoons melted shortening

Mix cranberries with powdered sugar and let stand while preparing the muffin mixture. Sift remaining dry ingredients. Add milk, egg and melted shortening. Stir only until the dry ingredients are moistened. Gently fold in the sugared cranberries. Pour into lightly oiled muffin pans, filling each 2/3 full, and bake at 350° for about 20 minutes or until done.

University of Alaska
Cooperative Extension Service

Sourdough Cranberry Muffins

1-1/2 cups unsifted all-purpose
   flour
1/2 cup wholewheat flour
3/4 cup firmly packed brown
   sugar
1 teaspoon salt
1 teaspoon baking soda
1 tablespoon powdered
   orange-drink mix

3 tablespoons powdered
   buttermilk
1/2 cup lowbush cranberries
1 slightly beaten egg
1/2 cup water
1/2 cup salad oil
3/4 cup sourdough starter

Mix all dry ingredients together in bowl and stir in the berries. In a separate container, blend together the egg, water and oil; stir in the sourdough starter, which must be thick to ensure the batter bakes properly. Pour into the flour mixture all at once. Stir just enough to blend ingredients. Fill greased muffin cups or paper liners about 2/3 full. Bake at 375° for 30 to 35 minutes.

Variations:
- Use 1/2 cup orange juice instead of powdered orange-drink mix and water.
- Use oatmeal or rye flour instead of wholewheat flour.
- Use 1/2 to 1 cup brown sugar to vary the sweetness of the muffins.

Mary Alice Sanguinetti
Naknek, Alaska

Blueberry Bannock

Sourdough pancake batter   Blueberries or huckleberries

Stir up your favorite sourdough pancake batter but make it extra thick. Mix in blueberries or huckleberries to suit your taste — not too many. Bake on a hot griddle, like pancakes, flipping several times to ensure that the bannock is thoroughly done. Eat while still warm or cooled. The bannock can be frozen and used later.

Hazel Vandeburgh
Anchorage, Alaska

Blueberry Pancakes

2 cups pancake mix	1 cup blueberries, drained (fresh,
2 cups milk	frozen or canned)
1 slightly beaten egg	Cinnamon and sugar, mixed
2 tablespoons melted butter	Butter or margarine
or margarine	Maple syrup

Add milk, egg and melted butter to the pancake mix and stir gently. Fold in well-drained berries. Bake on hot greased griddle. Turn cakes once to brown evenly on each side. Serve with cinnamon and sugar mix or with the more traditional butter and syrup.

Danish Pancakes

1/2 lemon	1 teaspoon salt
1/2 orange	1/2 teaspoon cardamom
1 peeled apple, cut in quarters	4 beaten eggs
2 cups lowbush cranberries	1-2/3 cups milk (room
1-1/2 cups maple syrup	temperature)
1-1/2 cups sifted flour	1/2 cup melted butter or margarine
2 tablespoons sugar	

For best results, the sauce should be made the day before this dish is to be served. To make sauce, first remove the seeds from the lemon and orange. Combine lemon, orange, apple slices and cranberries and run through a medium-bladed food chopper. Add the syrup and mix well. Chill. The next day, prepare the pancake batter. Sift together flour, sugar, salt and cardamom. Combine eggs, milk and butter, then add to the flour mixture, beating until smooth. To bake, spread 3 to 4 tablespoons on hot, ungreased griddle to make a 6-inch-round pancake. Once cooked, remove pancake from griddle, fold in half, then half again, to form a fan-shape. Place on a wire rack and keep hot in a slow oven until all pancakes are cooked. To serve, place 3 or 4 pancakes on plate with sauce.

Filled Pancakes

2 cups canned berries
1 cup sugar
2 slightly beaten eggs
1-1/2 cups milk

1 cup pancake mix
2 tablespoons melted butter
  or margarine

Combine berries and sugar in saucepan and bring to a boil. Reduce heat and cook 8 to 10 minutes. Keep berries warm while pancakes are being made. Combine eggs, milk, pancake mix and 1 tablespoon melted butter, stirring until smooth. Place remaining butter in a small fry pan and heat until bubbly. Pour in enough pancake batter to thinly coat the bottom of pan. Bake until lightly browned on underside. Flip the cake and bake on other side. Stack hot pancakes in a medium hot oven, leaving the door open, to keep warm. For serving, place 2 tablespoons warm berry mixture on each pancake and roll up like a jelly roll. Serve hot.

Snowflake Pancakes with Blueberries

1 yeast cake or 1/4-ounce
  package dry yeast
1/4 cup water
1 quart buttermilk
1 tablespoon baking soda
4 tablespoons sugar

1 teaspoon salt
4 cups flour
2 tablespoons baking powder
1/4 cup cooking oil
6 well-beaten eggs
1 cup blueberries

Preparation of these pancakes must begin the night before they are to be served. Soften yeast in warm water. (If using a yeast cake, water should be 80°. Dry yeast has better results if the water is heated from 105° to 115°.) In a separate container mix together buttermilk, baking soda, sugar and salt. Add to this the softened yeast. Sift flour and baking powder together and add, with the oil, to the buttermilk mixture. Mix well. Fold in the eggs. Place in refrigerator overnight in a container large enough to allow the batter to double in bulk. In the morning add the blueberries to the dough and stir down. Cook in a fry pan over medium heat and serve. This recipe will keep in a refrigerator for a week or more. If black specks appear in the batter, just stir them in. They are just the yeast mold and do no harm.

Lucile Preston
Kelso, Washington

Swedish Pancakes

Pancake batter

Canned lowbush cranberries

Make your own favorite pancake recipe or any of the ones listed in this book. Have griddle hot and greased. Pour 2 teaspoons batter on griddle for each tiny pancake. Bake as usual. Arrange 6 of the little pancakes around edge of plate and place a dab of canned lowbush cranberries on each. Lowbush Cranberry Sauce may be used instead. Sprinkle with powdered sugar.

Pancakes à la France

2 slightly beaten eggs	1 cup flour
1 cup milk	Raspberry or strawberry jam,
1/2 teaspoon salt	warmed slightly

Add milk, salt and flour to eggs and stir until smooth and evenly blended. Cover bowl and allow to stand for 1 hour. The batter should be extremely thin — just thick enough to coat a spoon dipped into it. Stir in a little more milk if necessary. Grease a small fry pan (5 to 6 inches is about right) with cooking oil. Pour in just enough batter to cover bottom of pan thinly. If there is a little too much batter in the pan, pour it back into the bowl, leaving a coating of batter in the fry pan. Cook on one side over moderate heat; turn with a spatula and cook on the other side until lightly browned. Spread jam on each pancake as it comes out of the pan and roll up the pancake. Serve as a dessert. Butter may be spread on the cakes before the jam if desired. These are best served warm.

Variation: Raspberry crêpes. Add 1/8 teaspoon salt to the batter. Add 1 tablespoon brandy to the raspberry jam. When all are prepared, sprinkle with sugar.

Alaska-Style Irish Bread

Baking powder biscuit mix	1 cup *dried* wild currants,
1-1/2 tablespoons salad oil	serviceberries or blueberries
2 tablespoons sugar	1 tablespoon dried rose hip powder
	1 tablespoon caraway seed

Follow your favorite recipe for baking powder biscuits and then add, in order given: salad oil, sugar, berries, rose hip powder and caraway seed. Stir just enough after each addition to mix well. Bake in an oiled, cast-iron fry pan for 25 to 30 minutes at 350°. Increase heat to 400° for the last 5 minutes. Serve warm with jelly or jam. This is a real treat for Sunday brunch.

Alaska Wild Berry Trails

Basic Cranberry Nut Bread

4 cups flour
2 cups sugar
3 teaspoons baking powder
1 teaspoon baking soda
1-1/2 teaspoons salt
2 oranges

4 tablespoons melted butter
  or margarine
Water
2 well-beaten eggs
4 cups lowbush cranberries
1-1/2 cups chopped nut meats

Sift together all dry ingredients, leaving a well. Grate off the orange-colored part of the rind from the oranges, then squeeze for juice. Combine butter, orange juice and enough water to make a total of 1-1/2 cups. Add the eggs to the liquid and pour into the well in the dry ingredients. Stir just enough to dampen completely. Fold in the cranberries and nuts. Fill well-greased loaf pans 2/3 full. Bake in a 350° oven for 40 to 80 minutes depending upon the size of pans used. Bread is done when it springs back when touched. This bread is better after it has been frozen a few weeks.

Variations:
  • Substitute wholewheat flour for half the white flour.
  • Substitute 1 cup candied orange peel for 1 cup berries.
  • Add 1 teaspoon nutmeg, 1/2 teaspoon allspice or cloves, or some of each.
  • Add 1 cup more nut meats or use pecans with walnuts or filberts.
  • Substitute dried wild berries for half the cranberries.
  • For a change, bake bread in muffin or ring pans.

Crab Apple Nut Loaf

3/4 cup Crab Apple Sauce
  (see recipe, page 137)
1 tablespoon dried orange peel
  (or bits)
2 tablespoons butter
  or margarine
1 slightly beaten egg
1 cup sugar

1/2 to 1 cup chopped dates
1/2 to 1 cup coarsely chopped nuts
1 cup white flour
1/2 teaspoon salt
1/2 teaspoon baking soda
1/2 teaspoon baking powder
Choice of spices
1 cup wholewheat flour

Heat applesauce, orange peel and butter together and set aside to cool. Blend egg and sugar together, adding dates and nuts. Combine with first mixture. Sift white flour with the salt, baking soda, baking powder and spices. Gradually add this, with the wholewheat flour, to the first mixture. Preheat oven to 325°. Spoon batter evenly into an oiled loaf pan lined with waxed paper. Bake for 45 to 60 minutes or until well done. Filberts are especially good in this loaf, but any nuts will do. Dried wild berries or raisins may be substituted for the dates.

Spicy Cranberry Bread

Juice of two large oranges
Water
6 tablespoons butter
  or margarine
2 tablespoons grated orange rind
  or dried orange rind
2-1/2 cups flour
1 teaspoon salt
1 teaspoon baking soda
1-1/2 teaspoons baking powder
1 teaspoon cinnamon

1 teaspoon nutmeg
1/2 teaspoon allspice
1/2 teaspoon ginger
1/2 teaspoon cloves
2 cups sugar
1 cup wholewheat flour
2 slightly beaten eggs
2 cups coarsely chopped walnuts
3 cups frozen lowbush cranberries
1/4 cup flour

Combine orange juice with enough water to make 1-3/4 cups total liquid. Bring to a boil. Add butter and orange rind; set aside to cool. Sift dry ingredients, with exception of wholewheat flour, into a large bowl. Mix in wholewheat flour. Make a well in the center. Set oven at 325°. Line loaf pans with strips of foil to fit. Pour cooled liquid into well in the bowl and stir in beaten eggs until moistened. Stir in chopped nuts. Remove cranberries from freezer at the last minute and spread quickly on a cookie sheet. Dredge with the 1/4 cup flour before the berries have a chance to thaw. Stir the floured berries into the batter quickly but gently being careful not to break the fruit. Fill pans half full with the prepared batter. Bake from 45 minutes to 1-1/2 hours depending on size of pans. Be sure to test for doneness since this bread is easy to underbake. Allow baked bread to cool on racks for 20 minutes. Remove from pans and peel off foil strips. Cool loaves completely before wrapping in foil and freezing. This bread will slice without crumbling if kept in the freezer until just before serving.

Spicy Cranberry Bread is an excellent holiday bread but should be made at least a month before using. It is better when allowed to ripen in freezer for a few weeks.

Variations:
  • Add 1/2 to 1 cup chopped candied orange peel to batter.
  • Substitute 1 cup brown sugar for 1 cup white sugar.
  • More walnuts make it even better.

Betty Ryan
Seattle, Washington

Coffee Break Cake

Biscuit mix   1 cup sugar
Lowbush cranberries

Mix coffee cake batter according to directions on biscuit mix package.
Turn batter into shallow, oiled baking pan and cover with a layer of
berries. Sprinkle the sugar over the berries. Bake slowly at 325° until
golden brown. Serve hot or cold, plain or with a topping. This is a good
recipe when you have only a few berries on hand.
Variation: Almost any firm, small-seeded berry will work in this recipe,
too.

Corinne U. Palmer
Olympia, Washington

Cran-Apple Breakfast Treat

2 cups flour   Lowbush Cranberry Jelly
3 tablespoons sugar   (see recipe, page 166)
3 teaspoons baking powder   2 to 3 peeled apples, cut into
Dash of salt   thick slices
1 cup whipping cream   Brown sugar
1 slightly beaten egg   Cinnamon
                                          Butter or margarine

Sift together flour, sugar, baking powder and salt. Whip the cream until
thick and carefully stir in the egg. Add whipped cream and egg to the
flour mixture and gently stir until dough forms a ball. Spread dough in a
well-oiled, 9-inch-square pan. Cover with a thick layer of jelly. Arrange
apple slices in rows on top the jelly and press firmly into place. Sprinkle
with brown sugar and cinnamon. Dot generously with butter. Bake at
400° for 30 to 35 minutes. Serve warm with a sauce of your choice.

Cranberry Sally Lunn

2 tablespoons butter or margarine   1/2 cup milk
3 tablespoons sugar   1 stiffly beaten egg white
1 egg yolk   1 cup fresh lowbush cranberries,
1 cup sifted flour   washed but not dried
2 teaspoons baking powder   Sugar
1/2 teaspoon salt

Combine butter and sugar and cream well. Add the egg yolk and beat
thoroughly. Sift together the flour, baking powder and salt and add,
alternating with the milk, to the butter-sugar-and-egg mixture. Beat well.
Carefully fold in the egg white. Pour into a well-greased baking pan. Roll
the damp berries in sugar and let stand a few minutes. Place baking pan

in oven at 400° for 5 minutes. Remove and sprinkle sugared berries generously over the top and continue baking for 15 to 20 minutes or until golden brown. Cut into squares and serve while still warm.

Lingonberry (Lowbush Cranberry) Coffee Cake

2 cups sifted, all-purpose flour
3 teaspoons baking powder
3/4 teaspoon salt
1/2 cup sugar
5 tablespoons butter
1 slightly beaten egg

1/2 cup milk
2-1/2 cups lingonberries
  (lowbush cranberries)
1/4 cup all-purpose flour
1/2 cup sugar
3 tablespoons butter or margarine

Sift together 2 cups sifted all-purpose flour, 3 teaspoons baking powder, 3/4 teaspoon salt and 1/2 cup sugar. Cut in butter until mixture is crumbly. Mix egg and milk; add to flour mixture, stirring slowly. Then beat until well blended. Spread batter evenly into an 8x8x2-inch, greased baking pan. Sprinkle berries evenly over the top of the batter. Combine 1/4 cup all-purpose flour with 1/2 cup sugar and cut in 3 tablespoons butter. Sprinkle this over the berries. Bake at 375° for 30 to 35 minutes. Serve warm.

University of Alaska
Cooperative Extension Service

North Star Scones

Red sugar (optional)
3/4 cup wild berry jelly or jam
1/2 cup finely chopped apple
  slices
3 tablespoons brown sugar
1/2 teaspoon cinnamon
1/4 cup chopped walnut meats

2 cups flour
4 teaspoons baking powder
1 tablespoon white sugar
Dash of salt
5 tablespoons butter or margarine
Egg white (or milk)

Prepare red sugar by stirring a few drops of red food coloring into granulated sugar. Prepare filling by combining jelly, apple slices, brown sugar, cinnamon and nuts. Blend lightly until mixture reaches spreading consistency. In separate bowl, sift together flour, baking powder, white sugar and salt. Blend in the butter. Roll out dough on waxed paper to about 10x20 inches. Spread filling over half the dough and carefully fold the other half of dough over the filling. Press edges firmly together with a floured fork. Transfer to ungreased baking sheet, waxed paper and all. Trim off excess paper and brush top of scone with egg white (or milk). Sprinkle the red sugar on top for a gala touch. Bake at 450° until golden brown. Cut into squares and serve warm.

Qwik Coffee Cake

3/4 cup sugar
4 tablespoons softened butter
  or margarine
1 egg
1/2 cup milk
1-1/2 cups flour

2 teaspoons baking powder
1/4 teaspoon salt
1/2 teaspoon almond extract
1/2 cup wild berry jam
1/2 cup finely chopped pecans

Combine all ingredients except jam and pecans and spread in an 8-inch-square pan, well oiled with vegetable oil. Place dollops of your favorite jam (wild strawberry is exceptionally good) over the top. Sprinkle with the chopped pecans. Bake at 350° for 30 minutes or until nicely browned.

Upside Down Rolls

1/4 cup butter or margarine
1/2 cup orange juice
1/2 cup sugar
2 teaspoons grated orange rind
1/2 cup chopped nut meats
1 cup blueberries
2 cups flour

1/2 teaspoon salt
3 teaspoons baking powder
3 to 4 tablespoons shortening
3/4 cup milk
Melted butter
1/4 cup sugar
Cinnamon

Combine butter, orange juice, orange rind and 1/2 cup sugar in saucepan and cook 2 minutes. Pour into greased muffin pans. Sprinkle on the nuts, then the fresh berries. Sift flour, salt and baking powder; cut in the shortening. Add milk and stir until dough follows fork around the bowl. Turn onto lightly floured board and knead for 15 seconds. Roll to 1/4-inch thickness. Brush with melted butter; sprinkle with 1/4 cup sugar and cinnamon. Roll up as for a jelly roll. Cut into 1-inch slices and place with cut side down over the mix in the muffin pans. Bake at 450° for 20 to 25 minutes.

SALADS AND DRESSINGS

Blueberry Nut Salad

Crisp lettuce leaves
2 medium oranges
2 cups fresh wild blueberries
1 cup filberts or other nuts
1/2 cup miniature marshmallows
1 cup whipping cream
1/4 cup fruit salad dressing
Nutmeg

Arrange lettuce leaves on salad plates. Peel the oranges and cut into thin slices; lay on one side of each plate in a fan shape. Mix berries, nuts and marshmallows and place a good-sized spoonful opposite the orange slices. Whip the cream and fold gently into the salad dressing. Put a dollop of the creamy dressing in center of each plate. Sprinkle with nutmeg and bits of nuts.

Blueberry Salad

1 3-ounce package cream cheese
1 pint whipping cream
1 cup miniature marshmallows
1 3-ounce package lemon gelatin
1 3-ounce package raspberry
  gelatin
1-3/4 cups boiling water
2 cups blueberry pie filling (see
  Blueberry Pie recipe, page 92)

Prepare topping the night before serving and refrigerate. Begin by breaking up the cream cheese into small bits; add it to the cream. Add the marshmallows. Prepare the salad the day of serving by first dissolving the gelatins in boiling water and then chilling until syrupy. Mix in the blueberry pie filling. Pour into a flat glass dish and chill until set. Just before serving remove the topping mixture from the refrigerator and whip until firm. Spread the topping thickly over the gelatin mixture. Cut into squares and serve on lettuce leaves.

Jane Helmer
Fairbanks, Alaska

Cottage Salad

1 envelope unflavored gelatin
1/4 cup cold water
2-1/2 cups Whole Berry
  Cranberry Sauce (see recipe,
  page 84)
2 teaspoons horseradish
1/4 teaspoon dry mustard
1/4 cup lemon juice
1 teaspoon grated lemon rind
1/4 teaspoon salt
Dash of cayenne
3/4 cup cottage cheese

Sprinkle gelatin over cold water in a small saucepan and on the lowest setting possible, heat for 3 minutes or until the gelatin dissolves. Add the cranberry sauce, then stir in the remaining ingredients, beating carefully to blend. Turn into molds rinsed in ice cold water. Chill until firm. Unmold and serve on crisp lettuce. This salad goes well with fish.

Cranberry-Orange Salad

2 cups lowbush cranberries
1 whole orange
1 cup sugar

1 package lemon gelatin
1 cup boiling water
1/2 cup cold water

Run cranberries through a food chopper. Quarter whole orange, remove seeds and put through a food chopper. Blend orange, cranberries and sugar. Dissolve gelatin in boiling water. Add cold water and chill until syrupy. Add cranberry mixture, pour into a mold and chill until firm. Serve on crisp lettuce leaves. This may also be used as a relish with poultry or other meat.

Cranberry Relish Mold

1 3-ounce package raspberry
  gelatin
1 cup Lowbush Cranberry Sauce
  (see recipe, page 83)

Lowbush cranberries
Sugar

Prepare gelatin following directions on package. When the gelatin begins to jell, carefully fold in the Lowbush Cranberry Sauce, then chill until firm. Just before serving, unmold onto a bed of mixed salad greens. Decorate with a few fresh, raw lowbush cranberries that have been moistened and dipped in sugar. Serve with your choice of fruit salad dressing.

Cranberry-Strawberry Salad

1 envelope unflavored gelatin
1/4 cup cold water
1 cup Lowbush Cranberry Juice
  (see recipe, page 142)
1 3-ounce package orange gelatin
1/4 cup sherry
1 cup strawberries, drained

1 cup finely chopped lowbush
  cranberries
1 cup commercial sour cream
1/2 cup walnuts
1 8-ounce package cream cheese
1/2 cup strawberry juice
2 tablespoons sugar

Dissolve unflavored gelatin in the cold water. Heat the cranberry juice just to the boiling point; remove from heat and stir in orange gelatin and dissolved unflavored gelatin; stir to dissolve completely. Add the sherry. Chill until thick and syrupy. Fold in the berries and sour cream until well mingled; add the nuts. Pour into a square baking pan and chill until set. Beat together the cream cheese (at room temperature), strawberry juice and sugar. Spread this mixture over the salad in the pan before serving. This may be sprinkled with finely chopped nuts if you wish. Cut in squares and serve on lettuce leaves.

Frozen Strawberry Salad

2 pints frozen strawberries   1 pint cottage cheese
1 pint sour cream

Thaw berries partially and mix with sour cream and cottage cheese. Pour into a ring mold and freeze until firm. Serve while still partially frozen. Fill center of ring with fresh fruits of any kind.

Hearty Luncheon Salad

1 envelope unflavored gelatin   1 recipe your favorite chicken
1/4 cup cold water   salad
2 cups Lowbush Cranberry Sauce   Toasted slivered almonds
   (see recipe, page 83)   White grapes
1 orange

Sprinkle gelatin over cold water in a small saucepan and place over low heat for 3 minutes or until gelatin is dissolved. Add to cranberry sauce and mix well. Cut orange into quarters, remove seeds and put rind and pulp through a food chopper. Add to the other mixture. Turn into individual molds rinsed in cold water. Chill until firm. Serve on double salad plates with chicken salad in one lettuce cup and cranberry salad in the other. Add a few toasted almond slivers to each and a few white grapes to the chicken salad for extra flavor.

Mary Taylor
Moose Pass, Alaska

Cranberry Mayonnaise I

1/4 cup Whole Berry Cranberry   1/2 teaspoon grated orange rind
   Sauce (see recipe, page 84)   1/2 cup mayonnaise
1 teaspoon lemon juice

Crush berries in the sauce with a fork. Gently blend sauce, lemon juice and grated orange rind into the mayonnaise.

Cranberry Mayonnaise II

1 cup whipping cream   1 cup mayonnaise
1 cup Lowbush Cranberry Jelly
   (see recipe, page 162)

Whip cream and carefully fold in mayonnaise and jelly. The jelly should be warmed just enough to soften, which is best done over hot water.

Cranberry Mayonnaise III

1 cup lowbush cranberries   1 cup mayonnaise
2 tablespoons powdered sugar

Crush berries with a fork. Fold the berries and powdered sugar into mayonnaise.

Creamy Currant Salad Dressing

1 3-ounce package softened cream   2 teaspoons lemon juice
  cheese   1/3 to 1/2 cup whipping cream
3 tablespoons Wild Currant Jelly
  (see recipe, page 168)

Whip the cream. Carefully blend in the remaining ingredients until evenly mixed. This dressing is good on almost any combination of fruits.

Dressing For Fruit Salad

1/2 cup your choice berry juice   Sugar
1/2 cup mayonnaise

Carefully mix the berry juice and mayonnaise or the dressing may curdle. Taste a sample and add sugar to suit your preference. This makes a lighter dressing than pure mayonnaise and is more suitable for fruit salads.

Enhancing Dressings For Salads

Start with 1 cup mayonnaise and blend in any of the following variations for fruit salad dressing:
- 1 cup chopped lowbush cranberries and a few drops orange juice.
- 1 cup Wild Currant Jelly (see recipe, page 168) and 1 cup whipped cream.
- Raspberry puree.
- 1 cup crushed strawberries, 1 tablespoon powdered sugar, 2 tablespoons lemon or orange juice, and 1 cup whipped cream.
- 6 tablespoons crushed strawberries or raspberries, 4 tablespoons toasted almonds (shredded), 2 tablespoons berry juice and 2 tablespoons white wine.

Strawberry Cream Mayonnaise

1 cup strawberries
1/2 tablespoon powdered sugar
3 tablespoons lemon juice

1 cup whipping cream
1 cup mayonnaise

Crush wild strawberries; add powdered sugar and lemon juice. Whip cream and fold into fruit. Carefully fold this mixture into the mayonnaise.

White Wine Dressing

1/4 cup fresh wild strawberries
1/4 cup finely chopped pecans
2 tablespoons berry juice

2 tablespoons white wine
1 cup mayonnaise

Crush berries and drain off juice. Add pecans, berry juice and white wine to the crushed berries. Fold carefully into the mayonnaise.
Variations: Use raspberries instead of strawberries and replace the pecans with toasted slivered almonds.

Wild Strawberry Salad Dressing

1/3 cup wild strawberry preserves
1/2 cup sour cream

1/4 cup mayonnaise

Lightly mix together the ingredients and serve on fruit salad. This dressing can be refrigerated in a covered container.

THE MAIN COURSE

—73

Baked Easter Ham

1 ham	1 teaspoon dry mustard
1 cup lowbush cranberry or other	1/2 teaspoon black pepper
berry syrup or jelly	1/2 cup orange juice
1 teaspoon cloves	2 tablespoons dried orange bits
1 teaspoon nutmeg	or grated orange peel
1 teaspoon allspice	1/2 cup hot water

Skin ham and remove any excess fat. With a sharp knife make holes into the ham 2 inches from one another and as deep as the bone. Do this on all sides. Boil the remaining ingredients together until a syrup is made. Force 1 tablespoon of this hot syrup into every hole in the ham, then place the ham in a large roasting bag. Place into a roaster. Pour half the remaining syrup over the ham, then close the bag, piercing several small hole in its upper side. Bake in a 325° oven for 18 minutes for each pound of ham. Brown the meat by slitting open the bag 30 minutes before it's through cooking. Pour the remaining syrup over the ham and finish baking.

Burger Steaks Royale

1-1/2 pounds ground game meat	Dash of Worcestershire sauce
or beef	5 or 6 tablespoons Lowbush
4 tablespoons butter or margarine	Cranberry Juice (see recipe,
Pinch of rosemary	page 142)
1/2 teaspoon dry mustard	

Form ground game meat or beef into oblong patties 3/4-inch thick. Melt 3 tablespoons butter in a large skillet. Add the rosemary to the butter for an extra touch of elegance. Place the patties in the butter and cook until as done as you like. Remove to a hot platter. Add the remaining 1 tablespoon butter and the Worcestershire sauce to the butter in the skillet. Stir in the dry mustard and the cranberry juice. Heat, but do not boil. When hot, pour over the burger steaks on the platter.

When making mincemeat of wild game use berry juice for a moistener.
After mincemeat has been prepared, add cranberry or currant (or any
other kind) jelly for any additional moisture needed.
Alaska Wild Berry Trails

Cranberry Catsup Meat Loaf

2 eggs	2 teaspoons horseradish
1-1/2 cups soft bread crumbs	3/4 teaspoon salt
1 cup chopped onion	1 teaspoon dry mustard
1/4 cup chopped green pepper	1/4 cup milk
1 pound ground moose or caribou	1/4 cup Highbush Cranberry
meat	Catsup (see recipe, page 86)
1 pound lean, ground pork	1 cup cranberry sauce

Preheat oven to 375°. Beat eggs in a large bowl; stir in the bread crumbs, onion and green pepper. Gently mix in the meat and pork. Mix together the horseradish, salt, mustard, milk and Highbush Cranberry Catsup; add this to the first mixture. Shape the whole into a round loaf and place on a sheet of foil in a shallow pan. Bake for 45 minutes or until well browned and crusty. A few minutes before the dish is finished baking, drain cranberry sauce and spread over the loaf.

Cranberry Meatballs with Mushroom Sauce

1 cup soft bread crumbs	1 teaspoon salt
1/2 to 3/4 cup crushed lowbush	1/4 teaspoon pepper
cranberries	Wholewheat flour
1/2 cup tomato sauce	A little shortening
2 eggs	1 10-3/4-ounce can mushroom
2 pounds ground beef	soup
1/2 to 3/4 cup quick-cooking rice	Milk or water
1/4 cup finely chopped onions	

Place crumbs in a large bowl; add berries, tomato sauce and eggs. Stir to mix and let stand until crumbs are well moistened. Mix in the ground beef, rice, onion, salt and pepper. Form good-sized meatballs and roll them in wholewheat flour. Cook with the shortening in a skillet until brown on all sides. Dilute the mushroom soup by half with milk or water, then pour over the meatballs. Cover and cook in 350° oven for 30 minutes. Turn the meatballs and cook for another 15 minutes uncovered.

Glazed Chicken

2/3 cup Lowbush Cranberry Juice	1/2 cup honey
(see recipe, page 142)	1/4 cup melted butter or margarine
1/2 cup prepared mustard	2 cut-up frying chickens

Stir together Lowbush Cranberry Juice, mustard, honey and butter. Place chicken pieces on a broiling pan and brush with juice mixture. Broil 6 to 8 inches from high heat, turning and basting with juice as necessary. Broil until tender, about 40 to 60 minutes.

Glazed Spareribs

Rack of pork *or* black bear spareribs	2 cups boiling water (about)
Salt	1 8-ounce can tomato sauce or paste
Pepper	1 cup Lowbush Cranberry Juice
Sage or thyme	(see recipe, page 142)

Preheat oven to 400°. Place ribs in shallow roasting pan and sprinkle with salt, pepper and sage or thyme. Add the boiling water and bake the ribs for 1 hour. Drain off the liquid. Combine the tomato sauce, cranberry juice and a pinch of salt. Pour this glaze over the ribs, making sure that the whole rack is completely coated. Reduce the oven heat to 350° and bake for another hour. Turn the ribs at least once and baste several times with the pan juice.

Alaska Wild Berry Trails

Ham and Dried Serviceberries

1-1/2 pounds center-cut, sliced ham	Pepper
1 cup *dried* serviceberries	1 cup brown sugar
3 medium-sized sweet potatoes or yams	2 cups scalded milk

Preheat oven to 350°. Place ham in a baking dish and cover with dried serviceberries. Peel the sweet potatoes, cut them lengthwise, and add to the ham and berries. Sprinkle with pepper and brown sugar. Add scalded milk. Cover and bake for 1 hour. Remove the cover and bake for another 30 minutes to brown the potatoes.

Moose à la mode

1 4-pound chunk of moose round or rump	2 tablespoons fresh or dried parsley
1 tablespoon salt	3 large, diced carrots
1/2 teaspoon black pepper	1-1/2 cups cranberry or currant jelly
2 sliced onions	

Place meat in large glass or pottery bowl and add all other ingredients. Cover and allow to stand in refrigerator overnight. The following day, remove moose from the liquid and strain out the vegetables if you wish. (I leave them in.) Return meat to the liquid, add more water if necessary and proceed as for pot roast. This is good cooked in a pressure cooker, too. Taste the liquid and add more seasoning if you think it needs it. Do not thicken this gravy; it is better thin.

Alaska Wild Berry Trails

Super Flank Steak

Flank steak from moose, caribou or other game
1/2 teaspoon salt
1/4 teaspoon pepper
2 tablespoons soy sauce
1/2 cup water or tomato juice
1/2 cup Lowbush Cranberry Sauce (see recipe, page 83)
1 tablespoon minced onion
1 tablespoon honey
Wholewheat flour

Score the steak diagonally on both sides. Mix all but the flour in a large flat dish. Marinate the steak for 2 hours or more, turning every half hour. Drain the steak well. Dredge in wholewheat flour and brown in a heavy skillet, turning as needed. When the meat is well browned, cut in 2-inch diagonal strips, sprinkle lightly with flour and add the marinade liquid. Cover and simmer slowly until most of the liquid is cooked away. Turn the strips and again sprinkle with flour and add a little water. Bake in a 350° oven, covered, until practically dry, turning once. You may need to add just a bit more water or tomato juice to keep the meat from scorching. This dish has a marvelous flavor.

Sweet and Sour Chops

1 teaspoon ginger
1 teaspoon salt
1/2 teaspoon pepper
1 teaspoon paprika
1/4 cup flour
6 thick-cut pork chops
1/2 cup raspberry juice
1/2 cup Rose Hip Juice (see recipe, page 142)
1 tablespoon shortening
2 teaspoons vinegar
1 tablespoon brown sugar
2 medium-sized tomatoes

Mix the ginger, salt, pepper, paprika and flour in a paper bag. Drop the pork chops into the bag and shake well to coat all sides with the flour mixture. Brown the chops in a skillet with the shortening. Mix the fruit juices together; add the vinegar; pour this over the pork chops. Sprinkle on the sugar, cover the skillet and simmer the chops slowly until they are tender, about 45 minutes. Serve with a tomato slice on top of each. The tomatoes may be broiled if you wish.

Sweet and Sour Ribs

2 pounds spareribs
1 tablespoon shortening
3 tablespoons brown sugar
3 tablespoons cornstarch

1/2 teaspoon salt
1 cup your choice berry juice
4 tablespoons vinegar
1 tablespoon soy sauce

Boil the spareribs for 1 hour or until tender. Drain and brown in a skillet with shortening. Add the berry juice, vinegar and soy sauce. Mix the sugar with the cornstarch and salt. Pour over the spareribs and simmer until the juice is slightly thickened.

MARINADES

Marinade for Broiled Flank Steak

1 teaspoon salt
1/2 teaspoon pepper
1 tablespoon soy sauce
1/2 cup minced chives
1/2 teaspoon garlic powder
2 tablespoons honey

1/4 cup water
3 tablespoons prepared mustard
1/2 teaspoon dill seed
1/2 cup Lowbush Cranberry Juice
(see recipe, page 142)

Mix all ingredients in a large, flat dish and marinate the flank steak for 3 hours, turning several times during the process. Broil the steak but not too well done. Slice on the diagonal for a tender steak.

Marinade for Fruits

1/4 cup orange juice
1/2 cup Lowbush Cranberry Juice
(see recipe, page 142)
1/4 cup blueberry or raspberry
juice
Grated rind and juice of 1 lemon

1/4 cup maple or corn syrup
1 vanilla bean or 1/4 teaspoon
anise seed
1/4 cup brandy or liqueur
(optional)

Thoroughly mix all ingredients. Pour over fresh fruits that have been peeled and then sliced, diced or quartered as required. Carefully mix the fruit and marinade. Cover and refrigerate for several hours.

Marinade for Game

1/2 cup vinegar
1/2 cup Lowbush Cranberry Juice
(see recipe, page 142)

2 finely minced garlic cloves
2 tablespoons salt
Cold water enough to cover meat

Mix ingredients in a bowl large enough to hold the marinade and game. Soak the game overnight. Use for any game, including game birds.

Marinade for Moose and Such

2 cups Lowbush Cranberry Juice
  (see recipe, page 142)
1 cup olive oil
2 large sliced onions
2 sliced carrots
2 mashed garlic cloves
1 teaspoon salt

1 bay leaf
2 tablespoons dried parsley
1/4 teaspoon thyme
8 peppercorns
1 clove
8 crushed juniper berries

Mix ingredients and pour into a bowl large enough to hold the marinade and meat. Marinate in refrigerator overnight, but longer is better. Turn the meat occasionally.

Marinade for Spareribs

1-1/2 cups Lowbush Cranberry
  Juice (see recipe, page 142)
1/2 cup tomato puree
1/4 cup tarragon vinegar
1/2 cup honey
1 large, chopped onion
2 cloves garlic, peeled and split

2 tablespoons Worcestershire
  sauce
1 tablespoon prepared mustard
2 teaspoons chili powder
2 teaspoons salt
Dash of Tabasco sauce
2 teaspoons oregano

Combine all ingredients in a large, flat dish and marinate the spareribs in the mixture for 24 hours in the refrigerator, turning frequently. This should be enough marinade for 5 or 6 pounds of ribs. Use the marinade for basting the ribs as they barbecue.

Cranberry Dressing for Pork

1/4 cup butter or margarine
1 cup diced celery
1 large diced onion
2 medium-sized apples, peeled
  and diced
5 cups dried bread cubes
1 teaspoon rubbed sage

3/4 teaspoon salt
1 cup Whole Berry Cranberry
  Sauce (see recipe, page 84)
1/4 cup brown sugar
Grated rind of 1 orange
1/2 cup orange juice

Melt butter and add celery, onion and apples. Stir over low heat until softened but not browned. Add bread cubes, sage and salt. Place cranberry sauce, brown sugar and orange rind in a saucepan and stir over low heat until sugar is dissolved. Add to the bread mixture. Gradually add orange juice, mixing until bread is moistened. This is a good stuffing for crown roast, or it may be baked separately for pork roast.

Cranberry Stuffing

1 cup lowbush cranberries
1/4 cup sugar
1/4 cup chopped celery
2 tablespoons chopped parsley
1/2 cup diced ham or bacon

4 tablespoons butter or margarine
3 cups stale bread crumbs
1 cup cornbread crumbs
Poultry seasoning to taste

Run the cranberries through a food chopper and add sugar. Cook celery, parsley and diced ham in butter for 5 minutes. Add the bread crumbs, seasoning and berries and blend lightly. This is particularly good with baked moose heart, wild duck or poultry.

Stuffing for Duck

3 cups wholewheat bread cubes
1/2 cup orange juice
1/2 cup ground lowbush
    cranberries
1/3 cup orange sections
    (membrane removed)

2 teaspoons grated orange rind
2 cups finely chopped celery
1/4 cup melted butter or margarine
1 slightly beaten egg
1/4 teaspoon salt
1/4 teaspoon pepper

Toast the bread cubes in the oven to ensure dryness. Add bread to juice and berries and let stand for 15 minutes. Add the remaining ingredients and toss lightly to mix. Stuff the bird and bake as usual.

Stuffing for Game Birds

10 slices of Basic Cranberry Nut
    Bread (see recipe, page 162)
3/4 cup hot water
Chicken bouillon powder or cubes
2 tablespoons butter or margarine

Salt
Your choice of additional
    seasonings
1 egg

Toast the bread slices in a slow oven to ensure dryness. Crumble into a bowl. Mix hot water and bouillon; add butter and wait for it to melt. Dampen crumbled bread well. Add salt and other seasonings to taste. Mix in the egg, unbeaten. This is an excellent stuffing for any game bird and goose in particular.

Variation: For a stuffing suitable for roast moose or caribou make a beef, rather than chicken, bouillon.

Lois Armstrong
Brookings, Oregon

Apple Horseradish Sauce

1 cup Crab Apple Sauce
  (see recipe, page 137)

1 4-ounce jar horseradish
1/2 pint whipping cream

Whip the cream. Combine all 3 ingredients and stir gently to blend. This is delicious with ham or other pork.

Bar-B-Q Sauce

1 cup Lowbush Cranberry Juice
  (see recipe, page 142)
1 cup catsup
1/2 cup water
1/4 cup Worcestershire sauce
1 large, chopped tomato

1/4 to 1/2 chopped green pepper
1/2 tablespoon minced, dried onion
  or equivalent in fresh onion
1 tablespoon horseradish
1-1/2 teaspoons dry mustard

Combine all ingredients in a saucepan and simmer for 10 minutes or so. This makes a good barbecue basting sauce for wild game, beef, lamb or pork.

Clear Cranberry Sauce

1 cup Lowbush Cranberry Juice
  (see recipe, page 142)
1 cup boiling water
1/2 cup sugar

1/4 cup orange juice
1 tablespoon horseradish
1 tablespoon prepared mustard

Mix Lowbush Cranberry Juice, boiling water and sugar and boil for 3 minutes. Add the orange juice and boil 2 minutes more. When this is nearly cold, gently stir in the horseradish and mustard. This is an excellent sauce for serving with ham. (Leave out the horseradish and mustard, and you have a hotcake syrup or dessert sauce.) It's best when served warm.

Cumberland Sauce for Game

1 cup Wild Currant Jelly
  (see recipe, page 168)
3 tablespoons prepared mustard
1 tablespoon minced onion
1/8 teaspoon ginger

2 tablespoons grated orange rind
1/2 cup orange juice
2 tablespoons lemon juice
1/2 cup Port wine
2 tablespoons cornstarch

Combine all ingredients, except for the Port wine and cornstarch, and stir to mingle. Cook over low heat, stirring frequently, until jelly is melted. Combine wine and cornstarch and mix well; stir it into the melted-jelly mixture. Cook, stirring, until sauce thickens. Serve hot or cold with game or other meat. (If reheating, be sure to stir the sauce continuously.) To store, keep in a covered container in the refrigerator.

Variation: Simple Cumberland Sauce. Combine 1 cup Wild Currant Jelly and 3/4 cup prepared mustard. Beat with an electric mixer until smooth.

Currant Ice

3/4 cup sugar
2 cups water

1 cup red currant juice

Combine sugar and water and bring to a boil; boil for 5 minutes. Blend in the currant juice and remove from heat immediately. Chill then freeze in a refrigerator tray without stirring. This is good with poultry or lamb.

Betty Ryan
Seattle, Washington

Deluxe Cranberry Sauce

1/2 cup shelled almonds
Ice water
2 cups sugar
1 cup water

1 pound lowbush cranberries
1/2 cup orange marmalade
Juice of 1-1/2 lemons

Blanch, peel and split almonds; soak them for 3 hours or more in ice water in the refrigerator. Mix sugar and 1 cup water in a large saucepan and bring to a boil without stirring. Simmer for 5 minutes, then add cranberries. Stir thoroughly once and cook for 3 minutes (or until all the berries have popped their skins) but no longer than 5 minutes. Remove from heat and add marmalade and lemon juice. Let stand until completely cool. Drain and sliver the blanched almonds; add them to the sauce. Serve well chilled.

Dried Berry Sauce

1 cup brown sugar
1 tablespoon cornstarch
Dash of salt
1/8 teaspoon powdered cloves
1 cup water
1 tablespoon vinegar

1/2 cup chopped *dried* berries or
  or rose hips or a combination
1 teaspoon grated lemon rind
1 tablespoon melted butter
  or margarine

Blend sugar, cornstarch, salt, cloves and water in a saucepan and cook slowly until sugar is dissolved, stirring constantly. Blend in vinegar, dried berries, lemon rind and butter. Cook again until well heated. Excellent with baked ham.

Lowbush Cranberry Sauce

4 cups lowbush cranberries
3 to 4 cups sugar
1 tablespoon orange juice

1 tablespoon grated orange rind
  or dried orange rind

Grind cranberries, using a medium blade and measure the 4 cups after grinding. Stir in the sugar and orange juice and rind. Allow to stand in a cool place and stir thoroughly every few hours for a day or two. No further processing is necessary. Put in sterilized jars and cover (do not seal). Store in a cool place or in refrigerator or freezer. If stored in freezer they should be in plastic containers instead of jars. There is so much acid in cranberries that they will keep for many months if stored properly.

Meatball Sauce

1/4 cup catsup
1/4 teaspoon garlic powder
1/2 cup Lowbush Cranberry
  Sauce (see recipe, page 83)

2 tablespoons butter or margarine
Orange juice (optional)

Blend together the catsup, garlic powder and Lowbush Cranberry Sauce. Place with butter in a saucepan and simmer for 5 minutes. Serve hot. The addition of orange juice provides a piquant taste. Try this as a dip sauce for those tiny cocktail meatballs.

Polish Juniper Berry Sauce

1-1/2 teaspoons juniper berries
2 tablespoons margarine
2 tablespoons wholewheat flour
1 cup beef bouillon

1/2 cup Madeira wine
Pinch of salt
Dash of pepper

Crush the juniper berries to a fine texture between several thicknesses of waxed paper, using a rolling pin. Heat the margarine until lightly browned. Gradually stir in the flour and cook over low heat, stirring constantly. Add bouillon and simmer for 15 to 20 minutes, stirring occasionally. Add the wine, salt, pepper and crushed juniper berries. Simmer again for 10 minutes or so. (You may need to add a little more bouillon if the sauce is too thick.) This sauce goes especially well with grouse or ptarmigan.

Sweet and Sour Sauce

1 8-ounce can crushed pineapple
1 green pepper, seeded and
  chopped
2 large chopped tomatoes
1 scant cup packed dark brown
  sugar
1 cup wine vinegar

1 tablespoon Worcestershire sauce
1 teaspoon dry mustard
1/2 cup Blueberry or Cranberry
  Syrup (see recipes, pages 154
  and 155)
3/4 cup water
2 tablespoons cornstarch

Combine pineapple, green pepper, tomatoes, sugar, vinegar, berry syrup, 1/2 cup water, Worcestershire sauce and mustard in a saucepan. Cover and simmer gently for 15 minutes, stirring occasionally. Blend the cornstarch into the remaining 1/4 cup water, then stir into the sauce slowly. Simmer until the sauce is thick and smooth.

Whole Berry Cranberry Sauce

6 cups lowbush cranberries
4 cups sugar

3/4 cup water

Blend all ingredients in a saucepan and bring to a full, rolling boil. Boil until a little of the juice will jell on the spoon, approximately 25 minutes. Pour into sterilized jelly glasses and seal.

Variations: For a change, try some or all of the following suggestions.
  • Substitute 1/2 cup honey for the same amount of sugar and reduce the amount of water used by 2 tablespoons.
  • Add slivered, crystallized ginger and/or a bit of grated orange rind.
  • Substitute a portion of orange juice for an equal amount of water.

Cranberry-Carrot Relish

1 8-ounce package dried apricots
6 medium-sized carrots
1 quart lowbush cranberries

4 cups sugar
2 cups water

Cut apricots into quarters or smaller. Shred the carrots. Combine all ingredients except carrots. Boil gently for 10 minutes, stirring occasionally. Stir in carrots and boil one minute longer. Spoon mixture into hot, sterilized canning jars. Seal and store in the refrigerator.

Florence Thornton
Rabbit Creek, Alaska

Cranberry-Horseradish Relish

Lowbush cranberries

Horseradish

Mix chopped, raw lowbush cranberries with grated horseradish in proportions of 2/3 cranberries to 1/3 horseradish. This goes well with cold meats. May be stored, covered, in refrigerator a month or so.

Cranberry-Mince Relish

2 cups Whole Berry Cranberry
  Sauce (see recipe, page 84)

1/4 cup Northland Mincemeat
  (see recipe, page 136)
1/4 cup chopped walnuts

Combine all ingredients and stir to blend. Chill for 1 hour or so before serving. This is especially good with game. Commercial mincemeat may be used if you have none of the wild berry variety on hand.

Cranlili

2 large green peppers
3 medium-sized onions
2 cups fresh lowbush cranberries

2 teaspoons salt
1 cup cider vinegar
1/2 cup sugar

Put peppers, onions and berries through a coarse-bladed food chopper. Add remaining ingredients and simmer slowly for 20 to 30 minutes. Pack in sterilized canning jars and seal immediately. Especially good on hot dogs and hamburgers.

University of Alaska
Cooperative Extension Service

Green Tomato Relish

2 quarts chopped green tomatoes
1/4 cup salt
1 cup rose hip puree
1 scant teaspoon pepper
1-1/2 teaspoons cinnamon
1-1/2 teaspoons dry mustard
1/2 teaspoon allspice

2-1/2 teaspoons ground cloves
1/4 cup white mustard seed
  (or 1-1/2 teaspoons more dry
  mustard)
1 quart cider vinegar
2 red or green peppers
1 large, chopped onion

Mix green tomatoes with salt and let stand for 24 hours or more. Drain thoroughly. Add remaining ingredients and stir to mix well. Bring to a boil and cook for 20 minutes on low heat — just barely bubbling. Pour into 1/2-pint or pint sterilized canning jars and seal immediately.

Variation: Add 1/2 cup brown sugar and your choice of spices to suit your family's taste. If you do, boil the mixture an additional 5 minutes.

Highbush Cranberry Catsup

6 pounds highbush cranberries
1-1/4 pounds sweet white onions
3 cups water
3 cups mild vinegar
6 cups sugar
1 tablespoon cloves

1 tablespoon cinnamon
1 tablespoon allspice
1 tablespoon salt
2 tablespoons celery salt
1-1/2 teaspoons pepper

Cook berries and onions in the water until soft. Put through a sieve and return the pulp to saucepan. Add remaining ingredients. Bring to a boil, reduce heat and cook until thick and catsuplike in consistency. Stir frequently to keep from sticking. Pour into sterilized canning jars and seal immediately. Process for 5 to 10 minutes in a boiling water bath. Use your Highbush Cranberry Catsup just like a regular tomato catsup.

Highbush cranberries are best when picked slightly underripe, for they become bitter as they ripen.

Lowbush Cranberry Catsup

1 pound lowbush cranberries
1/2 cup mild vinegar
1/2 cup water
1 cup brown sugar
1/2 teaspoon cloves
1/2 teaspoon ginger

1/2 teaspoon paprika
1 teaspoon cinnamon
1/4 teaspoon pepper
1/2 teaspoon salt
2 tablespoons butter or margarine

Boil the berries in the vinegar and water until they are soft. Put through a sieve. Add the sugar, spices, and salt and cook slowly for 4 or 5 minutes. Add the butter. Pour into sterilized jars, seal and process for 5 to 10 minutes in a boiling water bath. Serve at room temperature with pork or poultry.

Anna Marie Davis
Anchorage, Alaska

Rose Hip Catsup

1 quart rose hips
Cold water
2 cups cider vinegar
2 cups sugar
1 teaspoon onion powder
1/2 teaspoon black pepper

1/2 teaspoon dry mustard
1/2 teaspoon salt
Dash of cayenne pepper
1/2 teaspoon ground cloves
1/2 teaspoon cinnamon

Clean rose hips and place in saucepan. Barely cover with cold water, then bring to a boil. Simmer for 15 minutes or until soft. Put through a sieve to eliminate all seeds. Add the remaining ingredients and return to the saucepan. Cook over medium heat until thick, stirring now and then. Pour into sterilized bottles or canning jars and seal at once. Process for 5 to 10 minutes in a boiling water bath. Use like tomato catsup.

Alaska Indians and Eskimos often refer to cloudberries
(Rubus chamaemorus) *as salmonberries because of their salmon color. They are not the same berry as* Rubus spectabilis, *which is more commonly accepted as salmonberry over the extent of its range.*

Chutney Mit Beeren

1 1-pound, 14-ounce can fruit
cocktail
1/2 cup orange juice
1/2 cup sugar
1/4 cup light brown sugar
1/4 cup cider vinegar
1/4 teaspoon red pepper
1/2 teaspoon cloves

1/2 teaspoon salt
2 cups lowbush cranberries
1 cup chopped apples, unpeeled
1 tablespoon finely cut,
crystallized ginger
1 minced, small garlic clove
3/4 cup raisins

Drain the fruit cocktail, reserving 1-1/4 cups syrup. Mix syrup with orange juice, sugars, vinegar, red pepper, cloves and salt. Bring to a full boil, stirring frequently. Add the remaining ingredients and cook about 5 minutes, or until the berries pop their skins. Stir in fruit cocktail. Simmer slowly, stirring often, 15 to 20 minutes, or until the mixture thickens slightly. Pour into hot, sterilized canning jars and seal immediately. Process for 5 to 10 minutes in a boiling water bath. The chutney will thicken as it cools.

Cranberry Chutney

2 cups chopped lowbush
cranberries
1/2 cup seedless raisins
2 tablespoons finely chopped
onions or chives

1 cup brown sugar
2 tablespoons lemon juice
1 teaspoon salt

Mix all ingredients thoroughly. Place in refrigerator for several hours for flavors to mingle well. Serve with meat.

University of Alaska
Cooperative Extension Service

DESSERTS

If you've been baking long, you've no doubt developed a favored, time-tested pie pastry, but if not, or if you are looking for added convenience in cooking, consider the Master Mix for pie pastry, courtesy of the University of Alaska Cooperative Extension Service.

Master Mix

7 cups sifted all-pupose flour	1 pound lard (about 2 cups) or
4 teaspoons salt	other shortening (about 2-1/2 cups)

Mix flour and salt thoroughly. Cut in the lard or other shortening, using pastry blender, two knives or finger tips, until fat particles are no larger than small peas.

Use what you need and store the rest for a later date. If you're using lard in the recipe, store the Master Mix in the refrigerator. If you're planning to use other shortening, try one that does not require refrigeration, in which case the mix should be stored in an air-tight container.

8- or 9-inch Single Crust

1-1/2 cups Master Mix	2 to 3 tablespoons cold water

Sparingly sprinkle cold water over Master Mix, blending with fork. Let stand 5 minutes before rolling. Bake 10 to 12 minutes at 425°.

8- or 9-inch Double Crust or 10-inch Single Crust

2-1/2 cups Master Mix	4 to 6 tablespoons cold water

Combine and bake according to directions for one crust.

For the 9-inch crumb crusts mentioned in our pie recipes, we suggest the following:

Crumb Crust

1-1/2 cups graham cracker or vanilla wafer crumbs	1/3 cup melted butter or margarine 2 tablespoons sugar

Mix fine crumbs, margarine and sugar together thoroughly. (Use 3 tablespoons sugar for the graham cracker crumbs, 2 for the vanilla wafers.) Spread the crumb mixture evenly over a greased 9-inch pie pan, then pat into place to form a shell. A handy way to ensure an even crust is to press another 9-inch pie pan into the crumbs. Once the shell is formed, place in a 350° oven for 10 minutes.

Basic Wild Berry Pie

Pastry for double-crust 9-inch pie
1 cup sugar
1/4 cup sifted flour
Dash of salt

3 cups wild berries
2 tablespoons butter or margarine
1/4 cup cold water

Prepare pastry and line a pie pan with bottom crust. Sift together the sugar, flour and salt and sprinkle over the berries in a bowl; toss lightly to mix. (Tart berries may require more sugar.) Turn berry mixture into the pan. Dot with butter. Pour the cold water over the ingredients in the pan. Add top crust and crimp the edges to seal. Prick the crust to vent steam. Bake in a 450° oven for 10 minutes. Reduce heat to 375° and bake for another 30 minutes or until pie appears well done.

Hint: Place a sheet of foil somewhat larger than pie on shelf below it. *Most* berry pies boil over and make a mess in the oven and the foil will take care of that. (Foiled again!)

Berry Chiffon Pie

Graham cracker crust for 9-inch
  pie
2-1/4 cups fresh strawberries or
  raspberries
1/2 cup sugar
1 envelope unflavored gelatin
1/4 cup cold water

1/2 cup hot water
1 tablespoon lemon juice
Dash of salt
1/2 cup whipping cream
2 egg whites
1/2 cup sugar

Prepare graham cracker crust and press into pie pan. Bake at 350° for 10 minutes. Chill. Crush berries and sprinkle with 1/2 cup sugar. Allow to stand for 30 minutes. Soften gelatin in cold water, then dissolve in hot water. Allow to cool. Add the sweetened berries, lemon juice and salt to the gelatin; chill until partly set. Whip the cream until stiff and fold into the berry mixture. Beat egg whites until peaks form when beater is removed. Beat 1/2 cup sugar into egg whites and continue beating until peaks hold form. Carefully fold berry mixture into the egg whites and sugar. Pour combined mixtures into the crumb crust. Chill until firm. Garnish with extra berries.

Blueberry-Lemon Pie

1-1/4 cups ginger ale
1 3-ounce package lemon gelatin
1 pint vanilla ice cream
1 cup blueberries

1/2 cup sugar
Baked 9-inch pie shell
Slivered candied ginger

Prepare pastry and line pie pan. Boil ginger ale, then remove from heat. Dissolve gelatin in ginger ale. Immediately add ice cream and stir until melted. Chill until mixture holds it shape when dropped from a spoon. Combine blueberries and sugar. Carefully fold sweetened berries into the first mixture. Pour combined mixtures into the pie shell and refrigerate for several hours. Slivered candied ginger is good sprinkled on top.

Blueberry Pie

2 cups blueberries
1-1/4 cups sugar
1/2 cup water
2 tablespoons cornstarch

2/3 cup additional water
Baked 9-inch pie shell
Whipped cream

Mix berries, sugar and 1/2 cup water. Bring to a boil and simmer gently until the berries produce juice. Dissolve cornstarch in 2/3 cup water. Slowly add to the hot berries and cook gently, stirring all the while, until thick. Pour filling into pie crust. Chill. Cover with whipped cream.

Jane Helmer
Fairbanks, Alaska

Cloudberry Pie

Pastry for double-crust, 9-inch pie
3 cups cloudberries
1 cup sugar

3 tablespoons flour
2 tablespoons butter or margarine

Prepare pastry and line a pie pan with bottom crust. Gently mix berries, flour and sugar — be sure not to crush the berries — and pour into pie pan. Dot with butter. Place top crust on pie and seal edges. Bake in a 350° oven until crust is nicely browned.

Lois Armstrong
Brookings, Oregon

Variation: Serviceberry Pie. Substitute serviceberries for cloudberries. Add in 1/4 cup more sugar and 1 tablespoon each lemon juice and butter.

Barbara Maxwell
Rabbit Creek, Alaska

Cranberry Custard Pie

Pastry for single-crust, 9-inch pie
4 cups lowbush cranberries
1-1/4 cups sugar
3 well-beaten eggs

1/4 cup sugar
1/4 teaspoon salt
1/2 teaspoon cinnamon
1-1/4 cups scalded milk

Prepare pastry and line a pie pan with crust. Grind berries and add 1-1/4 cups sugar. Heat until sugar is dissolved, stirring all the while. Allow to cool thoroughly, then pour into pie shell. Prepare custard for filling by combining beaten eggs, 1/4 cup sugar, salt, cinnamon and scalded milk. Pour custard over the berry and sugar mixture. Bake at 450° for 10 minutes. Reduce heat to 350° and continue baking for 35 minutes or until pie appears done.

Barbara Johnson
Anchorage, Alaska

Cranberry Pie

Pastry for double-crust, 9-inch pie
3 cups lowbush cranberries
1-1/2 tablespoons cornstarch
1-1/2 cups sugar

Dash of salt
3 tablespoons water
1 teaspoon vanilla

Prepare pastry and line a pie pan with bottom crust. Combine the remaining ingredients in a saucepan and bring to a slow boil for 1 minute. Cool. Turn into the pie shell and cover with lattice pastry strips. Bake at 450° for 10 to 15 minutes, then reduce heat to 350° and continue baking for 30 minutes.

Cran-Raisin Pie

Pastry for double-crust, 9-inch pie
1 cup sugar
1 tablespoon cornstarch
Dash of salt
1/4 cup boiling water

Vanilla
3/4 cup seeded raisins
1-1/2 cups lowbush cranberries
Milk

Prepare pastry and line pie pan with bottom crust. Mix the sugar, cornstarch and salt. Add water, a few drops of vanilla and raisins. Beat until smooth. Add cranberries; stir until well mixed. Pour into the pie shell. Cover with top crust. Prick the crust to allow steam to escape. Brush the top crust with milk if you want a nice glaze. Bake at 425° for 10 minutes. Reduce heat to 350° and continue baking for 35 minutes or until pie appears done.

Cream-and-Sugar Berry Pie

Pastry for single-crust, 9-inch pie
4 cups fresh berries
2/3 cup sugar
4 teaspoons flour
1/4 teaspoon salt
1 cup whipping cream

Prepare pastry and line pie pan with bottom crust. Pour berries into pie shell. Mix together sugar, flour, salt and cream and pour over the berries. Bake at 350° until the crust becomes brown and the filling is set. Serve while still warm.

Virginia Culver
Chugiak, Alaska

Crowberry Pie

Baked 9-inch pie shell
4 cups fresh or frozen crowberries
1 cup sugar
1 tablespoon lemon juice
3 tablespoons cornstarch
Dash of salt
1/4 cup water
1 tablespoon butter or margarine
Whipped cream

Line the pie shell with 2 cups berries. Cook the remaining 2 cups berries with sugar, lemon juice, cornstarch, salt and water until fairly thick. Add butter and cool. Pour this mixture over the raw berries in the pie shell. Chill for 3 or 4 hours and serve with whipped cream or other topping.
Variations: Substitute 2 cups blueberries or 2 cups lowbush cranberries for half the crowberries. Use more sugar for cranberries.

Double-Good Blueberry Pie

1 cup sugar
3 tablespoons cornstarch
1/8 teaspoon salt
1/2 cup water
4 cups blueberries
1 tablespoon butter or margarine
1 tablespoon lemon juice
Whipped cream
Baked 9-inch pie shell

Combine sugar, cornstarch and salt in a pan. Add water and 2 cups blueberries. Cook until mixture boils and is thick and clear, stirring all the while. Remove from heat and stir in butter and lemon juice. Cool. Mix in remaining 2 cups uncooked blueberries and pour into pie shell. Serve with whipped cream.

Mrs. Ross Bradford
Creswell, Oregon

Glazed Strawberry Pie

1 quart strawberries	Dash of salt
1-1/4 cups sugar	2 egg whites
1/2 cup water	1/2 teaspoon vanilla
1/2 teaspoon cream of tartar	Baked 9-inch pie shell

Pour berries into the pie shell. Mix the sugar, water and cream of tartar in a saucepan, cover and bring to a boil. Uncover and continue cooking until the syrup "spins a thread." (Spoon up some syrup and slowly begin to pour it back into the pan from about 18 inches. If threadlike wisps flow from the spoon, the syrup is ready.) Add the salt to the egg whites and beat until stiff. Gradually pour the syrup into the egg whites. Continue beating until syrup and egg white mixture forms peaks. Stir in the vanilla. Pile on top of berries in the pie shell, leaving an uncovered center area. Allow to cool, but do not refrigerate.

Florence Thornton
Anchorage, Alaska

Kuchen

Extra rich pie pastry	1/2 teaspoon salt
4 tablespoons flour	1-1/2 cups additional sugar
2 cups your choice berries	1-1/3 cups evaporated milk
1 tablespoon sugar	1-1/3 cups water
3 eggs	

Prepare pastry and line a 7x11-inch pan. Sprinkle 1 tablespoon flour and 1 tablespoon sugar over the crust to prevent it from becoming soggy. Sprinkle berries over crust. To prepare custard, beat eggs, remaining flour, salt and 1-1/2 cups sugar with a mixing spoon. (Do not use a mixer.) Dilute the milk with water and stir into the first mixture. Pour custard ingredients over berries. Bake at 425° for 20 minutes. Reduce heat to 400° and continue baking for 25 minutes or until custard is set. Almost any berry or other fruit will work well in this kuchen.

Mrs. Ed Seyfert
Unalakleet, Alaska

A bit of lemon juice or rind adds to blueberry dishes. Orange juice or rind are natural complements in any cranberry recipe.

Nagoonberry Pie

3 beaten egg yolks
1 scant cup sugar
Pinch of salt
1 cup nagoonberry juice
1 envelope unflavored gelatin

3 egg whites
1/2 teaspoon cream of tartar
Whipped cream
Baked 9-inch pie shell

In a double boiler mix egg yolks, 1/2 cup sugar, salt and 1/2 cup berry juice. Place over boiling water and cook until mixture thickens (about 10 to 12 minutes), stirring gently as it cooks. Soften gelatin in the remaining 1/2 cup juice. Remove egg mixture from heat and stir in gelatin. Chill. Mix together the remaining sugar and cream of tartar. Beat the egg whites until foamy, then gradually beat in the sugar and cream of tartar. Continue beating until stiff. Fold the 2 mixtures together and pour into baked pie shell. Chill. When ready to serve, top with whipped cream.

Maxcine Williams
Eugene, Oregon

Pop-in-a-Pan Pie

4 quarts fresh blueberries
3-1/2 cups sugar
3/4 cup quick-cooking tapioca

6 tablespoons lemon juice
1 teaspoon salt
Pastry for double-crust, 9-inch pie

This recipe makes enough filling for four 9-inch pies; fillings can be stored for up to 6 months before use. To prepare filling, wash and drain berries, then mix well with sugar, tapioca, lemon juice and salt. Line four 9-inch pie pans with heavy-duty foil. Allowing the foil to extend 5 inches beyond the rim of each pan. Pour filling equally into foil-lined pans. Fold foil loosely over the tops and freeze until solid. Remove frozen filling from pans, fold foil tightly and return to freezer.

To bake the pie, prepare pastry and line 9-inch pie pan with bottom crust. Take filling from freezer and remove foil. Do not let filling thaw. Pop frozen filling into a pastry-lined pie pan and dot with butter. Add top crust, seal edges and cut slits in crust for vents. Bake at 425° until syrup boils up with heavy bubbles that do not burst.

Raspberry Fluff Pie

Vanilla wafer crust for 9-inch pie
1 tablespoon plain gelatin
1/2 cup cold water
1/2 cup sugar
1-1/2 cups crushed raspberries

1 tablespoon lemon juice
1 stiffly beaten egg white
1/2 cup chilled evaporated milk
1/3 cup softened cream cheese

Prepare a vanilla wafer crust. In top of a double boiler mix gelatin and 1/4 cup cold water and let stand 5 minutes. Add sugar and remaining cold water. Stir over boiling water until the gelatin and sugar dissolve; then remove from heat. Add crushed berries and lemon juice. Mix well, then chill until mixture starts to thicken. Carefully fold in egg white. Whip chilled evaporated milk and cream cheese together for 2 minutes, then fold into first mixture. Pour into pie shell and chill for at least 3 hours.

Rose Hip Crumble Pie

Pastry for single-crust, 9-inch pie
1 cup *dried* rose hips
1/4 cup milk
1-1/2 cups sifted flour
2 teaspoons baking powder
1-3/4 cups brown sugar

Dash of salt
1/2 cup shortening
2 beaten egg yolks
2 egg whites
Pecan halves (optional)

Prepare pastry and line a pie pan. Soften rose hips in milk. Sift together flour, baking powder and salt. Cream in shortening and brown sugar, mixing well. This makes a crumbly mixture — reserve 1 cup for topping. To the remainder, add the egg yolks, milk and rose hips. Beat the egg whites until peaks hold form. Fold into the berry mixture. Spoon into pie pan and sprinkle with the crumbly topping. Garnish with pecan halves, too, if you wish. Bake at 350° for 35 to 45 minutes or until pie appears well done.

Rose Hip Pie

Pastry for double-crust, 9-inch pie
1-1/2 cups rose hips (best if not
    quite ripe)
1/4 pound melted butter
1-1/2 tablespoons cornstarch

1 cup sugar
2 beaten eggs
1 cup light corn syrup
Dash of salt
1 teaspoon vanilla

Prepare pastry and line a pie pan with bottom crust. Clean and seed rose hips. Mix cornstarch and sugar and blend in melted butter. Add the eggs, corn syrup, salt and vanilla; mix. Stir in the rose hips. Pour into the pie shell and cover with a lattice crust. Bake at 350° until pastry is nicely browned.

Hint: A little lemon juice keeps this from being too blah. Rose hips are quite bland.

It only takes a few rose hips to give you all the Vitamin C value found in one orange. And the farther north they grow, the more Vitamin C the hips have.

Salmonberry Cream Pie

6 cups salmonberries
Water
2/3 cup sugar
3 tablespoons cornstarch

Dash of salt
Whipped cream
Baked 10-inch pie shell

Crush 2 cups berries and force through sieve. Add enough water to make 1-1/2 cups. Mix together sugar, cornstarch and salt and add to berries. Cook, stirring constantly, for 5 minutes or until the mixture is well thickened. Allow to cool. Place remaining 4 cups berries in pie shell, then pour on cooked mixture. Chill for several hours. Serve with whipped cream and garnish with a few perfect, whole salmonberries.

Strawberry Pie

1/2 pint whipping cream
1 heaping cup strawberries
3/4 cup sugar
2 tablespoons lemon juice

2 egg whites
1/4 teaspoon salt
2 baked 8-inch pie shells

Whip the cream and refrigerate. In a mixing bowl beat the remaining ingredients for 5 minutes. Fold in the whipped cream and pile into baked pie shells. Refrigerate for 6 hours. This works well with other berries, too.

Hannah Weber
Quincy, Washington

Yukon Cherry Pie

Pastry for double-crust, 9-inch pie
1-1/2 cups lowbush cranberries
1 cup sugar
1/4 teaspoon salt

1 teaspoon vanilla
1 cup water
4 to 5 tablespoons flour
1 slightly beaten egg

Prepare pastry and line a pie pan with crust. Cook the berries, sugar, salt and vanilla in the 1 cup water until the berries are soft. Thicken with a paste made from the flour and a little cold water. Allow to cool, then blend in the slightly beaten egg. Pour into crust. Cover with the top crust, which should be pricked for vents. Bake at 450° for 10 minutes. Reduce heat to 350° and continue baking until crust is well browned. This is a good substitute for cherry pie.

Wild Strawberry Pie

1 quart strawberries
Baked 9-inch pie shell
1 cup sugar

3 tablespoons cornstarch
Whipped cream

Place half the raw berries in the pie shell. Crush the remaining berries. Mix sugar with cornstarch and combine with the crushed berries. Cook until clear and thick. Cool and pour over the raw berries in the pie shell. Serve with whipped cream.

Mary Taylor
Moose Pass, Alaska

Berry Meringue "Tarts"

4 egg whites
1/2 teaspoon vinegar
1 teaspoon vanilla
Dash of salt
1/2 cup quick-cooking oatmeal

1 cup sugar
4 cups whipped cream
2 cups salmonberries,
   raspberries, strawberries, or
   cloudberries

Preheat oven to 275°. Cover a cookie sheet with plain white paper. Beat the egg whites; gradually add vinegar, vanilla and salt. Continue beating until frothy. Slowly add sugar, beating hard after each addition. Continue until the meringue stands in peaks. Gently fold in oatmeal. Make 7 or 8 mounds of the meringue on the paper-covered cookie sheet. Using a spoon, form hollows in the centers of the mounds and shape their sides until they look like tart shells. Bake 45 to 60 minutes. Allow to cool for an hour or more. Combine the whipped cream with the berries and fill the tartlike shells.

Gather wild berries in the afternoon of a sunshiny day if you can. Several hours of exposure to the sun before picking means more ascorbic acid in the fruit. It is also better than picking earlier when there is still dew on the plants. The berries will be wet and so will you if they are picked under those conditions.

Blueberry Pockets

1 cup fresh blueberries
3 tablespoons sugar
1-3/4 cups sifted flour
3/4 teaspoon salt
2-1/2 teaspoons baking powder
1/2 teaspoon cinnamon
1/8 teaspoon allspice

1/3 cup shortening
1 cup shredded wheat, crushed
   to crumbs
1-1/2 teaspoons grated or dried
   lemon peel
2/3 cup milk
Cream

Preheat oven to 450°. Butter 12 muffin cups. Combine berries and
2 tablespoons sugar. Let stand. Sift together flour, 1 tablespoon sugar, salt,
baking powder and spices. Mix in shortening until crumbly. Stir in cereal
crumbs and lemon peel. Add milk and stir until mixture holds together.
Knead lightly 10 times on a floured board. Roll to 1/4-inch thickness. Cut
into 3-inch squares and place squares in muffin cups. Fill with a heaping
tablespoon of berry mixture. Bring corners of dough together and press
edges together firmly, allowing to just fill the cups. Bake 20 minutes or
until brown and bubbly. Serve with real cream.

Hint: To form tart shells, roll out the pastry and cut it into 3-inch circles.
Press the circles over inverted muffin tins to shape. Remove the pastry
carefully, set the muffin tins upright and set the pastry inside. Now you're
ready to drop the filling in and bake!

University of Alaska
Cooperative Extension Service

French Strawberry Cream Tart

1-1/2 cups sifted flour
1/2 teaspoon baking powder
Dash of salt
1/2 cup butter
1 slightly beaten egg
1/2 cup sugar
2/3 cup sugar

4 tablespoons cornstarch
Dash of salt
2 cups milk
2 slightly beaten eggs
1/2 teaspoon vanilla
1/2 teaspoon lemon flavoring
2 cups strawberries

Preheat oven to 425°. Sift together flour, baking powder and a dash of
salt. Blend in butter until the mixture attains a mealy texture. Add
1/2 cup sugar to one slightly beaten egg and blend; stir into flour mixture
and mix well. Press dough into the bottom and sides of a greased 9-inch
pie pan. Bake about 20 minutes, then allow to cool. Combine 2/3 cup
sugar, cornstarch and a dash of salt in top of double boiler. Gradually stir
in the milk and cook over low heat, stirring constantly until mixture is
thick and smooth. Pour hot mixture slowly over 2 slightly beaten eggs,
then beat well. Return mixture to top of double boiler and cook over

boiling water for 5 minutes more, stirring all the while. Allow to cool, then stir in the vanilla and lemon flavoring. Put into cooled tart shell and arrange cleaned strawberries over the top of custard just before serving.

Glacé Strawberry Tarts

3/4 cup Rose Hip Juice
(see recipe, page 142)
2 tablespoons sugar

Pastry for 8 tart shells (see Master
Mix recipe, page 90)
2 cups wild strawberries

Boil Rose Hip Juice and sugar gently until thick and syrupy, then cook for 20 minutes more in the top of a double boiler over hot water, stirring now and again. Preheat oven to 450°. Cut pastry into circles large enough to fit over inverted muffin tins. Shape onto the tins and prick with a fork. Bake for 20 minutes or until shells are done. Cool before lifting from the tins. Just before serving fill the tart shells with strawberries. Spoon the glaze over the berries. Whipped cream topped with chopped nuts adds a nice decorative touch.

Mincemeat Tarts

1/4 cup dry sherry
1/2 cup dark corn syrup
1/4 cup butter or margarine
1-1/2 cups Cranberry
"Mincemeat" (see recipe,
page 135)

3 slightly beaten eggs
1/2 cup coarsely chopped pecans
Pastry for 8 tart shells
(see Master Mix recipe, page 90)
Whipped cream

Line 8 muffin tins with pastry. Preheat oven to 375°. Stir corn syrup, butter and sherry into the Cranberry "Mincemeat." Cook over medium heat until mixture comes to a boil, stirring all the while. Gradually stir in the beaten eggs and add pecans. Pour into the tart shells and bake for 25 to 30 minutes or until the tops of the tarts spring back when touched lightly. Allow to cool. Top with slightly sweetened whipped cream before serving. Northland Mincemeat does well in these tarts, too.

Highbush cranberries can be found on the bush even in the dead of winter. They provide a refreshing frozen treat to the hiker smart enough to pick the frozen berries.

Basic Wild Berry Cobbler

1/2 to 1-1/2 cups sugar (amount
   varies with tartness of berries)
1 tablespoon cornstarch
1 cup boiling water
3 cups your choice berries
1 tablespoon butter or margarine
Your choice of spices (optional)

1 cup sifted flour
1 tablespoon sugar
1-1/2 teaspoons baking powder
1/2 teaspoon salt
1/4 cup shortening
1/2 cup milk

Preheat oven to 400°. To prepare the fruit filling, combine sugar and cornstarch and blend in boiling water. Stir over medium heat until mixture has boiled for 1 minute. Add berries, then pour into a buttered 10x6-inch pan. Dot with butter and sprinkle on spices if you wish. Keep the berries warm in the oven while the topping is being prepared.

To prepare the topping, sift together flour, sugar, baking powder and salt. Work in the shortening, then stir in the milk until a soft dough is formed. Drop by spoonfuls over the hot berry mixture and bake for 30 minutes. Cobblers are great served with fruit sauces, milk or ice cream.

Simple Berry Cobbler

1/4 cup butter or margarine
1 cup flour
1 cup sugar

3/4 cup milk
2 cups your choice berries

Preheat oven to 350°. Melt butter in 1-1/2-quart casserole dish. Mix together flour, sugar and milk; pour over the melted butter. Do not stir. Sprinkle the berries over the batter. Bake for 30 minutes. Can be served warm or cold, plain or with whipped topping or ice cream.

Eleanor Prince
Wrangell, Alaska

Cranberry Cobbler

1-2/3 cups sugar
1/3 cup pancake mix
1 teaspoon grated lemon rind
4 cups lowbush cranberries

3/4 cup additional pancake mix
1 beaten egg
1/4 cup melted butter or margarine
Cream or ice cream

Preheat oven to 375°. Combine 1 cup sugar, 1/3 cup pancake mix and lemon rind. Add berries and toss lightly. Place in a 9-inch-square baking pan. Combine additional 3/4 cup pancake mix and 2/3 cup remaining sugar. Stir in the beaten egg until mixture resembles coarse crumbs. Sprinkle this evenly over the cranberry base. Sprinkle with melted butter and bake for 35 to 40 minutes. Serve with cream or ice cream.

Lucile Crocker
Elk City, Idaho

Juicy Huckleberry or Blueberry Cobbler

2-1/2 cups sugar
3 tablespoons butter or margarine
1 cup sifted flour
1 teaspoon baking powder
1/2 teaspoon salt

1/2 cup milk
1 quart fresh huckleberries
  or blueberries
1-1/2 cups boiling water
Ice cream

Preheat oven to 375°. Cream 1/2 cup sugar and 1 tablespoon butter together. Sift together flour, baking powder and salt. Add to sugar mixture. Gradually stir in the milk. Spread into a large, well-buttered baking dish. Cover batter with berries and dot with remaining 2 tablespoons butter. Sprinkle with remaining 2 cups sugar, then pour the boiling water over the top. Bake for 1 hour. Serve with ice cream.

Lillian Wisniewski
Depoe Bay, Oregon

PUDDINGS, STEAMED PUDDINGS AND TAPIOCAS

Alaskan Flan

2 tablespoons sugar
3 beaten whole eggs
3 beaten egg whites
1 13-ounce can evaporated milk

1 14-ounce can sweetened
  condensed milk
2 tablespoons vanilla extract
2 cups sweetened crushed
  salmonberries or cloudberries

Preheat oven to 350°. On a stovetop burner, cook the sugar, stirring constantly until sugar turns into a dark, caramel substance. Pour into a baking pan. Blend together the beaten whole eggs, egg whites and milks. Add vanilla, then pour into the baking pan with caramel and cover. Place covered pan into a second shallow baking pan half-filled with hot water. Bake for 2 hours. Serve cold with crushed berries poured over each serving.

Blueberries, huckleberries and bilberries are all closely related and belong to the family of heaths.

Berry Crumb Pudding

Tart berries
Bread crumbs

Butter or margarine
Sugar

Preheat oven to 375°. Place alternate layers of berries and bread crumbs into a buttered, deep baking dish. As each layer is added dot with butter and sprinkle with sugar. Top with a layer of crumbs. Cover and bake until berries are well cooked. Remove cover and continue baking a few minutes until crumbs are brown. Serve warm with dessert sauce or whipped cream.

Variation: Use blueberries and sprinkle in grated orange rind or dried orange bits.

Corinne U. Palmer
Olympia, Washington

Blueberries and Cognac Custard

3 slightly beaten egg yolks
4 tablespoons sugar
Dash of salt
1 cup scalded milk

1/2 teaspoon vanilla
2 to 4 tablespoons cognac or
   similar spirits
Blueberries

Begin by heating water in the lower part of a double boiler. Do not boil the water; overcooking will curdle the custard in this recipe. Place the slightly beaten egg yolks in the top of the double boiler and add the sugar and salt. Gradually add the scalded mlk, slowly stirring with a wooden spoon. Continue stirring until the mixture forms a coating on the spoon, at which time remove the custard from the heat and pour into a cool bowl. Add vanilla and enough cognac to suit your taste. Pour blueberries into individual bowls and cover with the custard.

Blueberry Buckle

2 cups flour
2 teaspoons baking powder
1/2 teaspoon salt
1/4 cup butter or margarine
1 cup sugar

1 slightly beaten egg
1/2 cup milk
2 cups blueberries
Cream
Graham cracker crumb topping

Combine flour, baking powder and salt. In another bowl, cream butter and sugar until light and fluffy. Add the egg and beat well. Now add flour mixture, alternating with milk, and beat until smooth. Fold in the berries and pour into a greased pan, approximately 9x9 inches. Sprinkle with a topping of graham cracker crumbs. Bake in a 375° oven for 30 to 35 minutes or until tests as done. Serve while still warm. Cut in squares and pass a pitcher of real cream.

Blueberry Delight

1 7-ounce package muffin mix
2 tablespoons melted butter or
   margarine
4 tablespoons packed brown
   sugar

1 diced banana
Blueberries
Chopped nuts
Cream

Preheat oven to 350°. Prepare muffin batter according to directions on package, then add melted butter and sugar. Pour the batter into a square, shallow baking pan. Sprinkle diced banana pieces, berries and chopped nuts generously over the batter. Bake until well browned. Cut into squares and serve while still warm with cream.

Variation: Substitute red huckleberries for the blueberries.

Hazel Vandeburg
Grants Pass, Oregon

Blueberry Pandowdy

4 cups blueberries
1 cup sugar
2 tablespoons lemon juice

1 15-ounce package yellow
   cake mix
Cream

Preheat oven to 375°. Combine blueberries, sugar and lemon juice and spread over a 9x9-inch pan. Prepare cake batter according to directions on package. Spread batter over the blueberry mixture in the pan. Bake for 20 to 25 minutes or until nicely browned. Cut in squares and serve warm with cream.

Blueberry Slump

4 cups blueberries
1-3/4 cups sugar
4 tablespoons cornstarch
1 teaspoon nutmeg
1/2 teaspoon cinnamon
3 tablespoons shortening

1/2 cup milk
1-1/2 cups sifted flour
1-1/2 teaspoons baking powder
1/4 teaspoon salt
Cream

Bring slowly to a boil the berries, 1-1/2 cups sugar, cornstarch and spices. While this berry mixture is heating, make the batter. Begin by creaming the shortening with the remaining 1/4 cup sugar, then add milk and blend thoroughly. Mix together the flour, baking powder and salt and stir into the shortening mixture. Drop batter by spoonfuls over the boiling blueberry mixture. Cover and cook at the same heat for 10 minutes. Serve hot and with cream.

Karen Clark
Cassiar, British Columbia

Crowberry Flummery

1 quart crowberries
1/2 cup hot water
1-1/4 cups sugar
Dash of salt

1 teaspoon lemon juice
2 tablespoons cornstarch
3 tablespoons cold water

Mix crowberries with hot water, sugar, salt and lemon juice and bring to a boil. Reduce heat and continue cooking slowly until a thin syrup is evident. Make a smooth paste of the cornstarch and cold water and stir into the crowberry mixture. Continue cooking until the mixture is slightly thick. Allow to cool. Serve with cream or over ice cream. Very simple but delicious.

Virginia Culver
Chugiak, Alaska

Danish Style Berries

4 cups your choice berries
2 cups water
Sugar

1/2 teaspoon vanilla
2 tablespoons cornstarch
Finely chopped almonds

Put 2 cups of your favorite wild berries in water and bring to a boil. Continue boiling gently until the juice has been extracted from the berries. Put the juice through a strainer and sweeten to taste. Place the remaining 2 cups of berries in the juice and cook until the berries are tender. Add the vanilla. Make a thickening agent by pouring a little of the hot juice into the cornstarch. Mix thickening into the boiling mixture. Add the finely chopped almonds and continue cooking until thick. Remove from the heat and sprinkle a little sugar on top to keep a crust from forming.

Anna Marie Davis
Anchorage, Alaska

New England Blueberry Pudding

3 cups blueberries
3/4 cup brown sugar
1/2 cup water
Butter or margarine

6 slices wholewheat bread
Cinnamon
Ginger

Mix together blueberries, sugar and water and cook for 10 minutes. Sparingly butter the bread slices, then lightly sprinkle each with cinnamon and ginger. Begin with the berries and alternate layer of berries and bread in a loaf pan. The last layer should be berries. Chill for 4 hours or more. Serve with preferred topping.

Raspberry-Rice Pudding

2/3 cup precooked rice
2 cups milk
1/3 cup sugar
1/2 teaspoon salt
1/8 teaspoon nutmeg

1/8 teaspoon cinnamon
1 to 1-1/2 cups whipped cream
1 16-ounce can cling peaches
1/3 cup raspberry jelly

Combine rice and milk in a saucepan and bring to a boil, then reduce heat, cover loosely and simmer for 15 minutes. (Fluff the rice occasionally with a fork.) Remove from heat and stir in sugar, salt and spices. Allow to cool for 5 minutes, then chill in your refrigerator's freezing compartment for 20 to 25 minutes. Do not allow it to freeze. Carefully fold rice mixture into whipped cream, then spoon into dessert dishes. Place a peach half, cut side down, on each serving of pudding. Melt jelly over hot water and dribble a little over each peach half.

Saucy Crunch

1 quart Whole Berry Cranberry
  Sauce (see recipe, page 84)
3/4 cup sugar
1 tablespoon orange juice
Dash of salt

1-1/2 cups corn flakes crumbs
4 tablespoons melted butter or
  margarine
Dash of ginger or 1 tablespoon
  crystallized ginger

Combine cranberry sauce, 1/4 cup sugar and orange juice in a saucepan and cook over medium heat for 5 minutes. Remove from heat and cover. Combine remaining 1/2 cup sugar with salt, ginger, crumbs and 2 tablespoons butter. Spread half the cranberry mixture over the bottom of a greased baking dish. Cover with half the crumb mixture. Repeat with the remaining cranberry sauce and crumb mixtures. Drizzle the remaining 2 tablespoons melted butter over the top crumb layer and bake at 350° for 25 to 30 minutes. Remove pan from oven, place on rack and allow to stand for 5 minutes before cutting into serving squares.

Huckleberry Roly Poly

1/3 cup butter or margarine	1 teaspoon baking powder
2/3 cup sugar	Dash of salt
2 well-beaten eggs	1/3 cup milk
2-1/4 cups flour	Red huckleberries, ripe but firm

Cream butter; stir in sugar gradually. Add eggs. Mix and sift flour, baking powder and salt. Add this, alternating with the milk, to the first mixture. Now gently stir in the red huckleberries. Pour mixture into 1-pound coffee cans until each is half-full. Cover with lids. Place on a rack in a large kettle of boiling water or in a steamer. Steam for 3 hours in boiling water. (Add water from time to time as it boils away.) Remove from kettle and set cans in cold water for 5 to 10 seconds. Turn cans upside down on a cookie sheet. Place the sheet in moderate oven for 10 minutes. Turn from cans, slice and serve with lemon sauce.

Variation: Instead of red huckleberries, use blueberries or lowbush cranberries.

Alaska Wild Berry Trails

Royal Plum Pudding

1/2 cup sifted flour	1/4 cup chopped walnuts
1/2 teaspoon baking soda	3/4 cup soft bread crumbs
1/2 teaspoon salt	1 cup ground suet
1/2 teaspoon cinnamon	1/2 cup brown sugar
1/2 teaspoon mace	2 well-beaten eggs
1/4 teaspoon nutmeg	1/4 cup Wild Currant Jelly
3/4 cup your choice *dried* berries	(see recipe, page 168)
3/4 cup *dried* wild currants	1/8 cup brandy
1/2 cup chopped citron	Lemon sauce
1/2 cup chopped candied orange peel	

Mix flour, baking soda and spices in a large bowl. Add fruits, nuts and crumbs, then blend in remaining ingredients and mix well. Pour into a greased mold until half-full. Place the mold in boiling water and boil for 6 hours, making sure the water outside the mold remains at all times as high as the mixture inside. Serve hot with lemon sauce.

Steamed Cranberry Pudding

2 cups lowbush cranberries	2 teaspoons baking soda
1-1/3 cups flour	1/2 teaspoon salt
1/4 teaspoon cinnamon	1/3 cup hot water
1/4 teaspoon mace	1/2 cup molasses
1/4 teaspoon cloves	Hard sauce

Mix cranberries and dry ingredients. Combine hot water and molasses and blend into the cranberry mixture. Place into well-greased pudding molds, cover and steam for 2-1/2 hours, making sure the water level outside the mold remains at all times at least halfway up the side of the mold. (Individual molds should be steamed for only 1 hour.) Serve with hard sauce.

Steamed Raspberry Mush

2 cups flour	4 cups cleaned raspberries
1 tablespoon baking powder	2 cups sugar
1 teaspoon salt	1 tablespoon lemon juice
1 tablespoon butter or margarine	Cream
3/4 cup milk	

Sift together flour, baking powder and salt, then work in the butter. Add milk and mix well. Combine berries, sugar and lemon juice and blend into the first mixture. Pour into a well-buttered mold, cover tightly and steam for 45 minutes, making sure the water level remains at all times at least halfway up the sides of the mold. Serve with cream.

Did you know that red raspberries are considered the most "elegant" of berries?

In Norway, rose hips are dried and sold in powdered form and are used in many ways. You can dry and powder your own in order to have Vitamin C all winter. There is not nearly as much vitamin as in the fresh rose hip but a lot is retained when dried or otherwise processed.

Old-Fashioned Blueberry Tapioca

1/2 cup pearl tapioca
6 cups cold water
3 cups blueberries
1 cup sugar
1 tablespoon cinnamon
1 teaspoon nutmeg

2 tablespoons lemon juice
2 tablespoons butter or margarine
1 grated lemon rind
Liberal dash of salt
Cream

Soak tapioca in 3 cups of water for 12 hours, then drain and rinse. Add another 3 cups fresh water and bring slowly to a boil, then simmer until tapioca is transparent. As tapioca simmers, gently mix together the remaining ingredients. Fold mixture into the transparent tapioca and cook for 5 minutes. Pour into a greased baking dish and bake at 350° for 45 minutes or until tapioca is lightly browned. Serve with cream, warm or cold.

Variation: Old-Fashioned Cranberry Tapioca. Use 2 cups fresh or frozen lowbush cranberries and 1 tart, peeled and chopped apple in the place of the blueberries. Use only 1/2 teaspoon cinnamon and 1/2 teaspoon nutmeg. A squirt from a "homestead" lemon or 1/4 cup orange juice replaces the grated lemon rind. Soak tapioca 8 hours at least.

Raspberry Tapioca

1/4 cup quick-cooking tapioca
1/2 cup currant or cranberry juice
3 cups water

2 cups fresh or frozen raspberries
Sugar
Dash of salt

Combine tapioca, water and juice and boil until tapioca is transparent. Add berries, sugar and salt to taste. Chill and serve cold with your choice of sauce.

CAKES, CUPCAKES, TORTES AND FROSTINGS

Alaskan Strawberry Delight

4 cups strawberries
1 cup sugar
1 3-ounce package strawberry
  gelatin

1 8-ounce package yellow cake mix
1 cup water
1/3 cup melted butter or margarine

Layer the berries in a greased 13x9-inch baking pan. Spread the sugar over the fruit; sprinkle the gelatin powder over this. Now scatter the cake mix, just as it comes from the package, over the gelatin. Drizzle the water over the ingredients in the pan. Do the same with the melted butter. Bake at 350° for 1 hour.

Ann Fitzpatrick
Medford, Oregon

Berry Roll

1 cup whipping cream	3/4 teaspoon baking powder
Dash of salt	Dash of salt
1 egg white	4 eggs
1/4 pound large marshmallows, cut in eighths	3/4 cup sugar
	3/4 cup sifted flour
2 cups strawberries, raspberries or salmonberries	1 teaspoon vanilla
	Powdered sugar

Prepare berry filling with enough time to let it chill before spreading over the cooled cake. To prepare the filling, whip cream until stiff. Combine salt and egg white and beat until peaks form. Fold marshmallows and whipped cream into the egg white mixture. Chill in refrigerator. To prepare the cake, preheat oven to 375°. Grease jelly roll pan and line with waxed paper. Mix baking powder, salt and eggs and beat hard for 1 minute. Add sugar gradually, beating until smooth. Stir in sifted flour and vanilla. Pour batter into pan and bake for 15 minutes or until cake tests done. Turn onto a towel covered with powdered sugar and peel off waxed paper. Roll up tightly in towel and let sit for 10 minutes. Gently unroll cake. When cake is cool remove filling from refrigerator and fold in the whole berries. Spread the filling over the cake and roll up again. Refrigerate until ready to serve.

Blueberry Cake

2 eggs, separated	1-1/2 cups flour
1/4 cup sugar	1 teaspoon baking powder
1/2 cup shortening	1/2 teaspoon nutmeg
1/4 teaspoon salt	1/3 cup milk
1 teaspoon vanilla	1-1/2 cups fresh or frozen blueberries
3/4 cup sugar	

Preheat oven to 400°. Beat egg whites until stiff. Add 1/4 cup sugar and continue beating until stiff again. Set aside. Cream the shortening; gradually add salt, vanilla and 3/4 cup sugar. Sift together flour, baking powder and nutmeg and add, alternating with the milk, to the shortening mixture. Carefully fold in beaten egg whites. Gently fold in the berries. Pour into a well-greased loaf pan and bake for 30 minutes or until cake tests done. Serve with lemon sauce, whipped cream or other topping.

Variations:
• Substitute half the white sugar with brown.
• Add finely cut, crystallized ginger and slivered almonds.
• Vary the amount of berries used.

Blueberry Cheesecake

12 crushed graham crackers
1/2 cup sugar
1/4 cup melted butter or
  margarine
2 well-beaten eggs
1/2 teaspoon vanilla
8 ounces cream cheese
1/2 cup sugar

1 quart fresh and firm blueberries
1/2 cup cold water
2 tablespoons cornstarch
1/2 cup sugar
1/2 teaspoon salt
1/2 teaspoon lemon juice
Whipped cream

This recipe should be prepared the night before serving. Preheat oven to 375°. Mix crushed crackers, 1/2 cup sugar and melted butter and press into 9x9-inch pan. Take the eggs, vanilla, cream cheese and 1/2 cup sugar and beat together until creamy. Pour over the crushed-cracker crust and bake 20 minutes. Crush 1 cup berries; add cold water, cornstarch, 1/2 cup sugar and salt. Cook until thickened. Add the lemon juice and remaining berries and heat until barely boiling. Cool and pour over cheesecake. Refrigerate overnight. Remove and serve with whipped cream or other topping.

Pacific Northwest
Blueberry Growers Association

Blueberry Sponge Cake

6 egg yolks
1 cup sugar
1/2 cup boiling water
1 teaspoon lemon extract
1-1/2 cups flour

2 teaspoons baking powder
1/2 teaspoon salt
4 cups crushed blueberries
1/2 pint whipped cream

Preheat oven to 325° to 350°. Beat egg yolks until light. Gradually add sugar and hot water, beating all the while. Stir in lemon extract. Sift together flour, baking powder and salt and add to first mixture. Beat well. Bake in 2 layer-cake pans for 25 minutes or a loaf pan for 45 minutes. Remove cakes from oven and allow to cool. Remove from pans. Mix blueberries and whipped cream (sweetened if desired) and place between the cake layers.

Mrs. William T. Foran
Seattle, Washington

Blueberry Upside Down Cake

1-1/8 cups cake flour
1/2 teaspoon salt
1-1/2 teaspoons baking powder
3/4 cup white sugar
1 egg

1/4 cup soft shortening
1/2 teaspoon vanilla
3 tablespoons butter or margarine
2/3 cup packed brown sugar
1 cup firm blueberries

Preheat oven to 350°. Combine flour, salt, baking powder and white sugar; sift, and mix with egg, shortening and vanilla. Melt butter in heavy skillet; sprinkle with brown sugar and cover with a layer of blueberries. Pour batter over this mixture and bake for 45 minutes. Turn out on serving dish. Should be served with whipped topping or berry sauce. Works well with other wild berries, too.

Virginia Culver
Chugiak, Alaska

Crab Apple Chocolate Cake

3 beaten eggs
2 cups sugar
1/2 pound butter or margarine
1/2 cup water
2-1/2 cups all-purpose flour
2 tablespoons cocoa
1/2 teaspoon salt

1 teaspoon baking soda
1 teaspoon cinnamon
1 teaspoon allspice
1 cup finely chopped walnuts
1/2 cup chocolate bits
2 cups crab apple pieces
1 tablespoon vanilla

Preheat oven to 325°. Cream together eggs, sugar, butter and water. Sift flour, cocoa, salt, baking soda and spices. Add to creamed mixture and blend. Fold in nuts, chocolate bits, crab apple pieces and vanilla until mixed well. Spoon into a greased and floured, loose-bottom tube pan. Bake 1 hour or until cake tests done. Serve while still warm.

There are several tests for "doneness" in baking.
Cakelike substances will spring back at once if touched lightly with
the finger tip. A thin bladed knife inserted into the baking dough
should come out clean with no dough adhering. Likewise with a
toothpick. Usually a nicely browned crust is an indication that the
dough is cooked to a turn but not always. Cranberry bread for
instance, may still be doughy inside when the crust is really well
browned, so be careful.

Crab Apple Sauce Cake

2 cups flour
2 tablespoons cocoa
1/2 teaspoon baking soda
1/2 teaspoon salt
1-1/2 teaspoons baking powder
1-1/2 teaspoons cinnamon
1/4 teaspoon cloves
1/2 teaspoon nutmeg

1/2 teaspoon allspice
3/4 cup coarsely chopped nuts
1/2 cup soft butter or margarine
1-1/2 cups sugar
2 eggs
1-1/2 cups Crab Apple Sauce
  (see recipe, page 137)
1 teaspoon vanilla

Preheat oven to 350°. Oil a 9x13-inch pan and line with waxed paper. Sift together flour, cocoa, baking soda, salt, baking powder and spices. Add nuts and toss to coat with the flour. In a large bowl, cream the butter and sugar until light. Add eggs, one at a time, while beating. Add flour mixture, alternating with apple sauce; add vanilla. Turn into prepared pan and bake for 50 to 60 minutes or until cake tests done. A coffee or mocha frosting is particularly nice with this cake.

Cranberry Angel Crown

1 15-ounce package angel food
  cake mix
1-1/3 cups Lowbush Cranberry
  Juice (see recipe, page 142)
1/2 cup butter or margarine
1 pound (approximately)
  powdered sugar

1/4 cup Lowbush Cranberry Juice
  (see recipe, page 142)
1/2 cup granulated sugar
1/4 cup water
2 cups fresh or frozen cranberries

Prepare cake mix, using 1-1/3 cups Lowbush Cranberry Juice instead of water. Bake as directed on the cake mix package. Cool cake in pan, upside down. To prepare frosting, cream butter in bowl until light and fluffy. Stir in 1/2 pound powdered sugar and about 1/4 cup Lowbush Cranberry Juice. Stir in portions of remaining powdered sugar until frosting is easy to spread. Put granulated sugar and water in saucepan and bring to a boil. Add cranberries and simmer over medium heat until berries are just tender. Remove from heat and cool. Drain berries and reserve the syrup. Place cake on serving dish and frost top and sides. Place the berries in a decorative border around base of cake and top edges. When ready to serve, drizzle syrup over the berries along edge of cake.

Cranberry Cake

1 cup shortening
1-1/2 cups sugar
4 eggs
2-1/2 teaspoons baking powder
3 cups sifted flour
Dash of salt
3/4 cup milk
1/4 cup orange juice

1/2 cup chopped walnuts
1 cup chopped dates
2 cups lowbush cranberries
2 tablespoons grated, dried orange peel
1 teaspoon chopped, crystallized ginger
Cranberry frosting

Preheat oven to 350°. Cream the shortening; add sugar. Add eggs, one at a time. Beat well. Sift the baking powder, flour and salt together. Combine milk and orange juice, and add to the shortening mixture, alternating with the dry ingredients. Fold in nuts, dates, berries, orange peel and ginger. Pour into a well-oiled and floured 10-inch tube pan and bake for 1 hour, 20 minutes or until well browned. When cake is almost cool, top with a cranberry frosting.

Cranberry Christmas Cake

1 15-ounce package white cake mix
2 teaspoons grated orange or lemon rind
3/4 cup finely chopped lowbush cranberries

Basic frosting
Holly leaves (real or imitation)
Whole cranberries

Preheat oven to 350°. Prepare the cake batter according to directions on the cake mix package. Add orange or lemon rind and blend well. Stir in the chopped cranberries and pour the batter into 2 round, 9-inch cake pans lined with waxed paper. Bake for 35 to 40 minutes. Cool. Tint a basic frosting pink and spread over cake. Garnish cake with holly leaves, using whole cranberries for holly berry clusters.

Lowbush cranberries or blueberries may be stored in rigid containers filled to overflowing with cold water and covered. In cold weather these berries may be poured into cloth bags and stored out of doors. Hang them up on nails to keep the pests away. Allow them to freeze and, kept frozen, they will keep all winter this way.

Easy Fruit Pudding Cake

2 tablespoons butter
1/4 cup white sugar
1 cup sifted flour
1 teaspoon baking powder
1/2 teaspoon salt
1 cup Crab Apple Sauce
  (see recipe, page 137)

6 tablespoons milk
1 cup packed brown sugar
1 teaspoon vanilla
Dash of ginger
1-3/4 cups boiling water

Preheat oven to 350°. Cream together butter and white sugar. Sift together the flour, baking powder and salt; stir in the Wild Crab Apple Sauce. Add the apple sauce mixture to the butter mixture, alternating with the milk. Turn batter into an oiled 2-quart casserole dish. Mix the brown sugar, vanilla, ginger and boiling water and pour over the batter. Bake about 30 minutes or until the top of pudding springs back when lightly touched. Serve upside down as this is a self-saucing dessert.

Icebox Cake

1 pound sponge or poundcake
2 cups strawberries or raspberries
2 tablespoons sugar
1/2 pint whipping cream

3 egg yolks
1 cup powdered sugar
1/2 teaspoon almond flavoring

Cut cake into 1/4-inch slices. Wash, hull and sprinkle the berries with sugar. Arrange a row of cake slices over the bottom of loaf pan and cover with sweetened berries. Add another layer of cake slices; then another of berries. Add a third layer of cake slices. Beat cream until thick and stiff. Beat egg yolks well and gradually add powdered sugar, beating until thick. Gently stir this mixture and almond flavoring into the beaten cream. Pour over cake and berries. Chill 3 to 4 hours before serving.

Peerless Raspberry Cake

1 package white cake mix
1 package raspberry gelatin
Sugar

2 to 3 cups raspberries
1 pint whipping cream

Prepare the cake mix according to directions on package and bake in a shallow rectangular pan. Prepare the gelatin as directed on the package and pour into another pan the same size as the cake pan. Chill. When the gelatin is set, unmold it onto the cake. Cover the whole thing with sweetened raspberries. Spread the top and sides with whipped cream or commercial topping. Cut into squares for serving.
Variation: Replace the raspberries with an equal amount of strawberries.

Lois Smith
Olympia, Washington

Qwik Cranberry Cake

2 cups Whole Berry Cranberry
   Sauce (see recipe, page 84)
1 stiffly beaten egg white

1 sponge cake
1 cup whipping cream

Beat cranberry sauce to break it down a little. Fold in the egg white. Slice sponge cake into 2 or 3 layers. Beginning with the cranberry sauce mixture, place alternating layers of sauce and cake in a mold, making sure that the top layer is cake. Place a weight on top (a plate with a few cans of food on top works well) and chill in the refrigerator for several hours. Unmold and decorate with whipped cream.

Raspberry Cake

2 cups sifted flour
1-1/2 teaspoons baking powder
1/2 teaspoon baking soda
1/2 cup shortening
1-1/4 cups sugar

3 eggs
3/4 cup buttermilk
1 teaspoon vanilla
2 cups raspberries
1/2 cup chopped walnuts

Preheat oven to 350°. Sift together flour, baking powder and baking soda. Cream the shortening and sugar; add eggs, one at a time, beating after each addition. Beat for 1 minute. Add to this the flour mixture, alternating with the buttermilk and vanilla. Fold in raspberries and nuts. Pour into 2 9-inch greased cake pans. Bake for 35 to 40 minutes. The cake may be served warm or cooled, topped with ice cream or whipped cream. Other wild berries work well in this recipe, too.

Hannah Weber
Quincy, Washington

Salmonberry Cake

2 cups flour
1 teaspoon baking soda
1/2 teaspoon salt
1 teaspoon allspice
1 teaspoon cinnamon
1 teaspoon nutmeg

1/4 cup butter or margarine
1 cup sugar
3 eggs
1 cup salmonberry jam
3/4 cup sour milk

Preheat oven to 375°. Sift together the flour, baking soda, salt and spices. Cream the butter and sugar together until fluffy. Beat the eggs until light and add to the sugar mixture. Blend the jam and sour milk together and stir into the egg mixture, alternating with the dry ingredients. Pour batter into 2 greased and floured cake pans. Bake 20 to 25 minutes. Ice with your favorite frosting.
Variation: Use raspberry jam in the place of salmonberry jam.

Spicy Cranberry Cake

1/2 cup shortening
1 cup brown sugar
1 beaten egg
3/4 cup chopped nuts
1 cup raisins
1-3/4 cups sifted flour
1/4 teaspoon salt
1 teaspoon baking soda

1 teaspoon baking powder
1 teaspoon cinnamon
1/2 teaspoon cloves
1 cup Whole Berry Cranberry
  Sauce (see recipe, page 84)
Cranberry Cheese Frosting
  (see recipe, page 121)

Preheat oven to 350°. Cream shortening and sugar. Add egg. Stir in nuts and raisins. Combine flour, salt, baking soda, baking powder and spices, sift and add to the shortening mixture. Gently stir in cranberry sauce so as not to break the berries. Pour into a greased tube pan and bake for 1 hour. Frost with Cranberry Cheese Frosting.

Upside Down Cake

1-1/2 cups lowbush cranberries
2 medium oranges
2 tablespoons butter or margarine
1 cup brown sugar
1-1/3 cups cake flour
2 teaspoons baking powder
1/4 teaspoon salt

1/4 cup shortening
1 to 2 teaspoons grated orange rind
3/4 cup sugar
1 egg
1/4 cup evaporated milk
1/4 cup orange juice
Nutmeg

Crush berries. Peel oranges and divide into sections, removing as much membrane as possible. Melt butter and stir in brown sugar. Mix and pour into a baking dish. Cover this with the cranberries and then with a layer of oranges. Sift together flour, baking powder and salt. Cream the shortening with orange rind; gradually add sugar, and beat until fluffy. Add egg and beat again. Mix milk, nutmeg and orange juice and add to the shortening mixture, alternating with dry ingredients, a little at a time. Pour the cake batter over fruit and bake in a 350° oven 40 to 50 minutes or until cake tests as done.

Blueberries and cranberries may be picked into large pails, but soft fruits such as raspberries and thimbleberries should be collected in small containers as they crush easily.

Blueberry Cup Cakes

1/3 cup butter or margarine
1/2 cup firmly packed brown
  sugar
1/2 cup granulated sugar
1 egg
1-3/4 cups sifted flour
1 teaspoon baking powder

1/4 teaspoon salt
1/4 teaspoon nutmeg
1/4 teaspoon cinnamon
1/2 cup milk
1 cup blueberries, (if frozen,
  defrost first)

Preheat oven to 350°. In mixing bowl, cream together butter and sugars until light and fluffy. Add egg and beat well. Sift together the flour, baking powder, salt, and spices. Add to creamed mixture, alternating with the milk, and mix until blended. Carefully add the blueberries, distributing them evenly throughout the batter. Fill paper-lined cup cake pans half-full. Bake for 20 to 25 minutes. Top with plain sugar frosting or serve with whipped cream or ice cream.

Hannah Weber
Quincy, Washington

Currant Cup Cakes

3/4 cup butter or margarine
1-1/4 cups sugar
4 eggs
2-1/2 cups sifted flour
1/4 teaspoon nutmeg

1/8 teaspoon salt
1 tablespoon baking powder
3/4 cup cleaned currants
3/4 cup milk
1 teaspoon vanilla

Preheat oven to 350°. Cream the butter; beat in the sugar and eggs thoroughly. Mix together flour, nutmeg, salt and baking powder; add the currants. Gradually add the dry ingredients and the milk to the creamed mixture. Add vanilla and mix well. Fill paper cups in muffin pans half-full. Bake for 20 minutes.

It is a good idea to pick a few rose hips with each container of berries, no matter what kind. Then when you process the berries the rose hips can be cleaned and processed with them for that extra dose of vitamins.

Wild Rose Petal Cup Cakes

1 cup sugar
1/2 cup butter (or vegetable
 shortening)
3 eggs
Grated peel of 1 lemon
3 cups cake flour

2 teaspoons baking powder
1/2 teaspoon salt
1 cup milk
1 cup cut, fresh wild rose petals
1 teaspoon lemon juice

Cream together the sugar and butter. Add eggs and beat well. Add the lemon peel. Combine the flour, baking powder and salt; sift and add to the first mixture, alternating with the milk. Add the rose petals. Finally, stir in the lemon juice. Line muffin pans with pink paper baking cups and fill each half-full of batter. Bake at 375° for 12 to 15 minutes.

Florence Thornton
Rabbit Creek, Alaska

Blueberry Breakfast Torte

1-1/2 cups sifted flour
2 teaspoons baking powder
3/4 cup white sugar
1/2 teaspoon salt
1/4 cup melted butter or
 margarine
2/3 cup milk

1-1/2 teaspoons vanilla
2 teaspoons grated or dried lemon
 rind
1 egg
1-1/2 cups wild blueberries
3 tablespoons melted butter
1/2 cup brown sugar

Preheat oven to 350°. Combine flour, baking powder, white sugar and salt. Add the 1/4 cup melted butter, milk, vanilla and 1 teaspoon grated lemon rind. Beat hard by hand. Add egg and beat hard again. Place in a well-greased, square pan. Mix berries, 3 tablespoons melted butter, brown sugar and remaining 1 teaspoon lemon rind. Dribble this mixture over the batter in the pan. Bake for 40 minutes. Cool and cut into squares to serve.

Anna Marie Davis
Anchorage, Alaska

Orange-Cranberry Torte

2-1/4 cups flour
1 cup granulated sugar
Dash of salt
1 teaspoon baking powder
1 teaspoon baking soda
1 cup chopped walnuts
1 cup diced dates
1 cup lowbush cranberries

Grated or dried orange rind
2 slightly beaten eggs
1 cup buttermilk
2/3 cup cooking oil
1 cup orange juice
1 cup powdered sugar
Whipped cream

Preheat oven to 350°. Sift together flour, granulated sugar, salt, baking powder and baking soda. Stir in nuts, dates, berries and orange rind. Combine eggs, buttermilk and oil, and add to the flour mixture, stirring until well blended. Bake in a tube pan for 1 hour or until done. Let stand for 1 hour. Remove torte from pan onto a rack placed over a wide plate. Combine orange juice and powdered sugar and pour over the torte. Gather drippings to pour over again. Set in a dish deeper than the torte. Wrap the whole in foil and refrigerate for 24 hours. Serve as is or with whipped cream.

Cranberry Cheese Frosting

1 3-ounce package cream cheese
4 tablespoons Lowbush Cranberry
  Sauce (see recipe, page 83)

1/8 teaspoon salt
1 pound powdered sugar

Soften cream cheese and mix with Lowbush Cranberry Sauce and salt. Gradually stir in powdered sugar until frosting is creamy in texture. This is not only a good cake icing, but it is wonderful spread on graham crackers for an after-school treat.

Jewel Cake Frosting

3-1/2 cups sifted powdered sugar
1/2 cup softened butter or
  margarine
2 egg yolks
1 teaspoon grated lemon rind
1 tablespoon lemon juice

1/8 teaspoon salt
1/2 cup finely chopped nuts
Red food coloring (optional)
3/4 cup lowbush cranberries
Whipped topping

Mix sugar, butter, egg yolks, lemon rind, lemon juice and salt until light and fluffy. Stir in nuts, 1/2 cup cranberries and a few drops of red food coloring. Fill and frost the cake. Garnish with a whipped topping and the remaining cranberries.

Florence Thornton
Rabbit Creek, Alaska

Sour Cream Frosting

1 cup sour cream	1 cup *dried* wild berries
1 cup sugar	Dash of salt

Combine all 4 ingredients in the top of a double boiler. Cook over hot water until thick, stirring occasionally. This is rich, and you may prefer to use it only as a filling between layers, while frosting your cake with another icing.

Strawberry Cake Filling

1/3 cup powdered sugar	1/2 teaspoon vanilla
2 cups whipped cream	Dash of salt
1 stiffly beaten egg white	1/2 cup crushed strawberries

Gently fold powdered sugar into whipped cream; fold in the stiffly beaten egg white. Add the vanilla and salt and blend well. Fold in the strawberries and fill your cake.

Variation: Try this with either wild raspberries or nagoonberries.

SHORTCAKES

Blueberry Shortcake

1 15-ounce package yellow cake mix	4 cups blueberries
2 teaspoons pumpkin pie spice	2 teaspoons grated or dried orange rind or bits
2 slightly beaten eggs	2 3-3/4-ounce packages vanilla pudding
1 cup water	

Combine cake mix, spice, eggs and water. Beat until smooth, then spread evenly into a greased and floured baking pan. Sprinkle 2 cups berries and all the orange rind over the batter. Bake as directed on the cake mix package. Remove from pan and cool. Prepare the pudding mix as directed on the box, then cool. Fold the remaining 2 cups berries into the pudding. Cut the shortcake into squares and split each into 2 layers. Spoon the pudding between and on top of the layers. Serve with a berry sauce.

Use whipped cream cheese as a topper for wildberry shortcake.

Cranberry Shortcake

2 cups flour
1/2 teaspoon salt
4 teaspoons baking powder
1 tablespoon sugar
1/2 cup shortening
1 well-beaten egg
1/2 cup milk
Melted butter

1 cup ground raw lowbush
  cranberries
1 cup tart, pared and ground
  apples
1/4 cup crushed and drained
  pineapple
1 cup sugar
Dash of salt

Preheat oven to 350°. Sift together flour, 1/2 teaspoon salt, baking powder, and 1 tablespoon sugar. Cut in shortening until the mixture is crumbly. Combine the egg and milk and stir into the first mixture just enough to moisten well. Turn onto a lightly floured board. Divide dough in half and pat out each half to fit an 8-inch round layer cake pan. Brush with melted butter and top with remaining round. Bake at 350° until shortcake appears done.

Combine cranberries, apples, pineapple, 1 cup sugar and dash of salt. Let stand 2 hours, then spread generously between and on top the shortcake rounds. Cut into wedges and serve with a favorite topping.

Variation: Salmonberry Shortcake. For the berry mixture, use 3 cups salmonberries, 3/4 cup sugar and 1 tablespoon lemon juice. Clean and crush the berries. Add lemon juice and sugar and stir gently, then let stand for 15 minutes for the berries to absorb the lemon juice and sugar. Spread salmonberry mixture between and over the shortcake rounds and serve in wedges with cream.

Berries do not always ripen the same place every year so keep searching for that extra good patch. They don't always ripen at the same time, either, because of the variations in seasons.

Strawberry Shortcake

3-1/2 cups flour
3 teaspoons baking powder
1/2 teaspoon salt
1/4 teaspoon nutmeg
3 tablespoons sugar
1/2 cup chilled shortening

1 well-beaten egg
1/4 cup milk
Soft butter or margarine
Sweetened strawberries
Sweetened whipped cream
Perfect, whole strawberries

Preheat oven to 400°. Grease 2 cookie sheets. Mix and sift dry ingredients twice. Cut in the shortening until mixture is crumbly in texture. Combine egg and milk. Make a well in the flour mixture and add the liquids, mixing lightly with a fork. A little more milk may be needed to make a soft dough that is a little stiffer than biscuit dough. Turn onto a lightly floured board and knead gently a few seconds. Roll dough to 1/2 inch in thickness and shape into 3-inch rounds with cookie cutter. Arrange on cookie sheets, several inches apart, and brush with milk. Bake for 15 minutes or until well browned. For serving spread butter over warm rounds and place on serving plates. Pour the strawberries over half the rounds and cover with remaining rounds and more berries. Top with a spoonful of whipped cream and garnish with a perfect berry or two.

Virginia Hetland
Olympia, Washington

COOKIES AND BARS

Alaskan Easter Bonnets

Finely chopped nuts
Wild berry jelly or jam
Wild berry juice

Powdered sugar
Vanilla
Sugar cookie dough

Prepare a basic sugar cookie dough and roll thin. Cut dough into 3-inch rounds. To prepare the filling, mix nuts in with jelly or jam. Place a teaspoonful of the jelly or jam mixture onto half the dough rounds. Cover with the other rounds. Carefully seal the edges by pressing with a floured fork, allowing no juice to escape. Bake on a greased cookie sheet in a 350° oven for 10 minutes or until cookies are light brown. While the cookies are still warm from the oven, accentuate the humps made by the jam, thus forming a "crown" for the bonnet. Decorate with an icing made of wild berry juice, powdered sugar and vanilla. Make bows, flowers or whatever. A little practice will produce elegant Easter bonnets.

Alaskan Hermits

1/2 cup margarine
1/2 cup sugar
1/2 teaspoon salt
2 well-beaten eggs
1/2 cup molasses
2 cups flour
1 teaspoon baking powder
1 teaspoon cinnamon
1/2 teaspoon cream of tartar

1/2 teaspoon cloves
1/4 teaspoon nutmeg
1/4 teaspoon mace
1/4 cup raisins
1/4 cup *dried* wild currants or
    serviceberries
3 tablespoons finely cut, candied
    orange peel
1/2 cup nuts (more if desired)

Cream together margarine and sugar; add salt, eggs and molasses and beat well. Combine 1-3/4 cups flour, the baking powder and spices and sift; add to the first mixture. Mix the raisins, berries, orange peel and nuts; sprinkle with 1/4 cup flour and toss to coat ingredients. Add to first mixture. Drop batter from a teaspoon onto oiled cookie sheets. The batter should be quite thin, spreading out well on the pans — leave about 2 inches of space between each. Bake in a 350° oven for 15 minutes, or until cookies are firm.

Berry Oatmeals

1/2 cup butter or margarine
1-1/2 cups sugar
1/2 cup molasses
2 well-beaten eggs
1-3/4 cups flour
1 teaspoon baking soda

1 teaspoon salt
1 teaspoon cinnamon
2 cups rolled oats
1 cup *dried* watermelon berries
3/4 cup coarsely chopped nuts

Preheat oven to 375°. Blend together butter, sugar, molasses and eggs. Combine flour, baking soda, salt and cinnamon; sift twice, then stir into first mixture. Mix in rolled oats, berries and nuts. Drop by teaspoonfuls on oiled cookie sheet. Bake for 10 to 12 minutes or until well browned.
Variation: If you've no watermelon berries on hand, use *dried* salal or serviceberries.

In the early 1970's nagoonberries were sold by an Alaska preserve company for about $45 a pint!

Berry and Rose Hip Macaroons

3/4 cup your choice *dried* berries
1/4 cup crushed, *dried* rose hips
7 ounces sweetened condensed
   milk
1/4 teaspoon salt

2 cups crushed cornflakes
1/2 teaspoon vanilla
1 cup shredded coconut
Dried orange bits

Preheat oven to 300°. Butter cookie sheets. Mix all ingredients together and shape into small balls with your fingers. Place dough balls on cookie sheets and bake for 10 minutes. Allow to cool for 2 to 3 minutes before removing from cookie sheets.

Cranberry Bars

2-1/2 cups graham cracker
   crumbs
1/2 cup melted butter or
   margarine
1 3-ounce package black cherry
   gelatin

1/2 cup sugar
1 teaspoon lemon juice
1-1/4 cups boiling water
2 cups whipping cream
1/2 to 3/4 cup lowbush cranberries

Preheat oven to 350°. Combine graham cracker crumbs and butter, blending well. Press mixture into bottom of 9x9-inch pan. Bake for 20 minutes. Mix gelatin, sugar and lemon juice. Dissolve in 1/4 cup boiling water. Add the remaining boiling water. Chill until gelatin is almost set but not yet firm. Whip cream and add berries; fold into the gelatin and spread on the cooled graham cracker crust. Refrigerate at least 3 hours. Cut into bars or squares for serving.

Fruit-Nut Cookies

1/2 cup butter or margarine
1-1/2 cups brown sugar
2 slightly beaten eggs
2 tablespoons sour milk
1/2 cup chopped walnuts
1 cup finely chopped, *dried* wild
   currants

1/2 cup your choice of another
   dried berry, chopped
1/2 teaspoon nutmeg
1/2 teaspoon cinnamon
3 cups sifted flour
1 teaspoon baking soda

Preheat oven to 350°. Combine butter and 1/4 cup brown sugar. Blend in eggs and milk slowly. Gradually add remaining sugar, then the walnuts, berries and spices. Combine flour and baking soda and gradually add to the first mixture, beating after each addition. Drop dough from a teaspoon onto greased cookie sheets. Bake for 15 minutes or until edges are brown. Remove from oven and allow to cool a little before slipping off the sheets.

Glazed Cookie Squares

1 17-ounce package refrigerated cookie dough	Assorted wild berries
	1/2 cup orange marmalade
8 ounces whipped cream cheese	2 tablespoons water

Preheat oven to 375°. Cut cookie dough into 1/8-inch-thick slices. Line a cookie sheet with foil and place the slices on the foil so they overlap slightly, making a rectangle approximately 14x10 inches. Press overlapping portions slightly to seal. Bake for 10 to 12 minutes or until browned. Cool and remove foil. Spread cream cheese over the crust and sprinkle generously with wild berries. Blueberries and salmonberries make a nice combination. Mix marmalade and water and quickly heat together. Glaze the top of the cookie rectangle with this mixture and chill for several hours. Cut into squares or bars.

Jam Rolls

Pie crust mix	Wild berry jam
Butter or margarine	Chopped walnuts or pecans

Preheat oven to 450°. Make dough according to instructions on pie crust mix package. Roll out on a lightly floured board. Cut into strips about 3x5 inches. Spread with butter and then with jam. Sprinkle chopped nuts over the jam and roll pieces like miniature jelly rolls. Bake 20 to 25 minutes or until golden brown. Jams rolls are a welcome addition to any lunch box.

Lois Armstrong
Brookings, Oregon

RECIPE FOR RELAXATION

1 golden day in Autumn
1 good friend
2 large pails
2 or more sandwiches

1 Thermos of your favorite
beverage
1 large blueberry patch (lowbush
cranberry patch will do)

Take the good friend to the berry patch on this lovely autumn day. As you gather berries be sure to keep up a continuous loud chatter to discourage bears. Fill your pails — although it doesn't really matter whether they are full or not. Pick until pleasantly tired then wend your way homeward with the fruit. See Remedy for Cabin Fever for what to do with the berries after you reach home.

Linzer Schnitten

3 eggs
2-1/4 cups sugar
3/4 cup melted butter or
  margarine
3-1/2 cups flour
1 teaspoon baking powder

1/4 teaspoon salt
1 teaspoon powdered cloves
2 teaspoons cinnamon
Grated rind and juice of 1 lemon
Strawberry preserves

Beat 2 eggs until light. Gradually beat in 1-1/2 cups sugar. Add melted butter. Sift together the flour, baking powder, salt and spices and blend into the butter mixture. Add lemon rind and juice. Turn dough onto a floured board and knead until smooth. Let stand for 2 or more hours. Roll dough to a 1/2-inch thickness and cut into 1-1/2x10-inch strips. With the handle of a wooden spoon, make a groove down the middle of each strip. Fill the groove with strawberry preserves, and place strips on a greased cookie sheet. Bake at 375° until brown — about 15 minutes. Beat together remaining egg and 3/4 cup sugar. Spread this glaze over the baked strips while they're still hot. Cut at once into diagonal pieces or squares. Linzer Schnitten is a super holiday confection!

Russian Diamond Cookies

1 cup *dried* wild berries
  (commercial dried currants
  work well, too)
1 cup chopped, seedless raisins
1 cup blanched and chopped
  almonds

1 cup chopped walnuts
1 cup chopped dried apricots
1 cup wild berry jam
2 eggs
Grated rind of 1 lemon
2 cups sifted flour

Preheat oven to 300°. Mix together all ingredients except flour. Sprinkle the flour over the mixture and blend thoroughly. Spread dough evenly over a buttered, 1/2-inch-deep cookie sheet. Bake for 30 to 40 minutes. Remove from oven and cool slightly. Cut dough into diamond shapes. Return pan to oven for about 5 minutes to dry out the cookies.

When gathering wild berries keep a separate container for odds and ends of berries that can all be thrown in together. Mixed berries can be used for syrups, jams, jellies and sauces. Often you may find only a handful each of several kinds and not enough to keep separate containers for each.

Strawberry Bars

2 cups sifted flour
1/2 teaspoon ginger
1/4 teaspoon salt
3/4 cup butter or margarine
8 ounces cream cheese

1 beaten egg yolk
3/4 cup strawberry preserves
1 beaten egg white
Sugar

Combine flour, ginger and salt; blend in butter and cheese. Mixture should be crumbly. Stir in egg yolk and knead resulting dough until smooth. Divide dough into thirds. Form each third into a rectangle. Chill 2 hours or more. On a lightly floured surface roll out each chilled rectangle, then place on greased cookie sheet. Form a strip down one side of each rectangle with 1/4 cup berry preserves. Brush egg white along sides of dough and fold over to form a long, enclosed bar. Cut slits in the top and crimp edges by pressing with a floured fork. Brush top with egg white and sprinkle lightly with sugar. Bake at 375° for 20 minutes. Let stand to cool, then cut into 1-1/2-inch bars.

Blueberry Dessert

2 cups blueberries
1/2 cup sugar
1 3-ounce package strawberry
  gelatin

1 cup boiling water
1 cup cold water
1 cup whipping cream
1/2 cup finely chopped pecans

Combine berries and sugar and cook slowly for 5 minutes or until syrupy. Chill. Dissolve gelatin in the boiling water. Add the cold water and stir to mix. Chill gelatin until syrupy. Fold half the berry mixture into half the gelatin and pour into parfait glasses. Chill until firm. Chill the remaining gelatin until firm, then beat until fluffy. Fold in the remaining berry mixture. Whip the cream and fold it in, together with the chopped nuts. Pour over the layer already in the parfait glasses and chill until firm. Top with 2 or 3 large blueberries.

A few fresh, unsweetened blueberries or raspberries added to ice cream just before serving make an especially appealing dessert in warm weather. Sweeten them a bit if you must but they are most refreshing if unsweetened.

Crab Apple Mousse

1 cup Crab Apple Sauce
  (see recipe, page 137)
6 tablespoons sugar
1-1/2 teaspoons grated lemon
  peel

Generous dash of nutmeg
Dash of salt
1 cup whipping cream

This recipe requires a cold refrigerator, so turn yours to its coolest setting. Mix Crab Apple Sauce, sugar, lemon peel, nutmeg and salt. Whip the cream and fold it into the Crab Apple Sauce mixture. Pour into a refrigerator tray and freeze for at least 2 hours. Turn into a chilled bowl and beat well. Return to refrigerator tray and freeze until firm.

Cranberry Loaf

2 cups Lowbush Cranberry Sauce
  (see recipe, page 83)
2 tablespoons lemon juice
1/2 pint whipping cream

1/4 cup powdered sugar
1 teaspoon vanilla
2/3 cup chopped pecans
  or walnuts

Combine cranberry sauce and lemon juice and turn into a refrigerator tray. Do not fill more than halfway. Whip the cream, then fold in the sugar, vanilla and nuts. Spread this over the cranberry layer and freeze untl firm. This may be prepared for a party several days ahead and kept frozen. Just slice at the last minute for serving.

Easy Frozen Dessert

1 cup whipping cream
3 ounces marshmallow whip

3/4 cup your choice crushed
  berries
1/4 cup chopped nuts

Whip the cream until stiff and fold in marshmallow whip. When these are gently but thoroughly blended, fold in the crushed berries and nuts. Pour into a refrigerator tray and freeze. This easy dessert has a velvety texture and is especially good served between waffles with fruit syrup on top.

Mrs. Westcott Gaines
North Little Rock, Arkansas

Fresh Berry Ice Cream

4 cups half-and-half
2 cups cold water
2 14-ounce cans sweetened
  condensed milk

2 tablespoons vanilla
3 cups your choice crushed berries

Chill all ingredients for 2 hours. Freeze in whatever type ice cream maker you have, following instructions for that particular freezer. For a less expensive ice cream use 6 cups of whole milk to replace the half-and-half and water.

Frozen Strawberry Custard

2 beaten egg yolks   .
1-1/4 cups powdered sugar
1 tablespoon lemon juice

2 cups fresh strawberries
2 egg whites
1/2 cup whipped cream

Combine the egg yolks with 3/4 cup powdered sugar, beating constantly for a creamy consistency. Combine lemon juice with berries and stir into the egg yolk mixture. Mix the egg whites with remaining 1/2 cup sugar, beating until stiff. Fold egg whites and whipped cream into fruit mixture. Place in a freezer until firm. Allow to stand at room temperature for 5 to 10 minutes before serving.

Lowbush Cranberry Parfait

1 envelope unflavored gelatin
6 tablespoons sugar
2 egg yolks
1-1/2 cups milk
1 teaspoon vanilla

2 8-ounce packages softened
  cream cheese
2 egg whites
2 cups canned lowbush
  cranberries (chilled)

Combine gelatin and 2 tablespoons sugar in a saucepan. Beat egg yolks with milk, then add to gelatin mixture. Stir over low heat until gelatin dissolves, about 5 minutes, then add vanilla. Beat cream cheese in a bowl until smooth, then gradually beat in gelatin mixture. Chill, stirring occasionally, until mixture forms a mound when dropped from a spoon. Beat egg whites until soft peaks form, then beat in the remaining 4 tablespoons sugar until stiff. Fold this into the cheese mixture. Alternate layers of cheese mixture and berries in parfait or other dessert dishes. Chill until set. You may need to add extra sugar.

Lowbush Cranberry Sherbet

2 cups lowbush cranberries	1 teaspoon unflavored gelatin
1-1/2 cups cold water	Juice of 1 lemon
1 cup sugar	

Cook the cranberries in 1-1/4 cups cold water for about 5 minutes. Stir frequently while cooking. Put berries through a fine sieve to make a puree. Return the puree to the saucepan and add the sugar. Stir over medium heat until all the sugar is dissolved, then simmer gently for 5 minutes more. Soak the gelatin in the remaining 1/4 cup cold water for about a minute or until the gelatin dissolves. Add the lemon juice to the gelatin. Stir the gelatin into the berry puree and allow to cool. Freeze in ice-cube trays until hard. Remove from refrigerator and break into small chunks in bowl of electric mixer. Beat until the mixture is mushy, allowing plenty of air to build up in the sherbet. Put into ice-cube trays again and freeze until firm. This is excellent with fruit salad on a hot day.

Raspberry Ice

2 quarts wild raspberries	2 cups water
2 cups sugar	1 tablespoon lemon juice
Dash of salt	

Clean berries as needed and sprinkle with the sugar. Cover and allow to stand for 2 hours or so. Crush berries thoroughly and force through a fine sieve. Stir in the remaining ingredients and freeze in a refrigerator tray. **Variation:** Substitute strawberries for the raspberries.

Lois Smith
Olympia, Washington

Raspberry-Mallow Dessert

2 cups miniature marshmallows	2 cups raspberries
1 cup milk	25 graham cracker squares
1 pint whipping cream	

Put marshmallows and milk in top of double boiler; melt over hot water. Whip the cream and fold in berries. Combine with marshmallow mix. Crumble graham crackers. Line a 10x13-inch pan with 3/4 of the crumbs. Pour in the filling. Sprinkle remaining crumbs on top. Chill. This may be prepared ahead of time and kept frozen. Remove from freezer an hour before serving.

Hannah Weber
Quincy, Washington

Strawberry Baked Alaska

4 egg whites	1 quart vanilla ice cream
1/8 teaspoon cream of tartar	Crushed and sweetened
1/2 cup sugar	strawberries

Beat together egg whites and cream of tartar until stiff peaks are formed, then gradually beat in sugar. Set the vanilla ice cream on several thicknesses of heavy brown paper on a small board. Make a fair-sized hollow in the ice cream and fill it with the crushed strawberries. Cover with the beaten egg-white meringue, being sure to seal the edges of the ice cream to the paper. Keep this dessert frozen until ready to serve, then pop it into a 450° oven until the meringue is lightly browned, about 5 minutes. *Watch it closely.*

Strawberry Ice Cream

1 pint strawberries	1 teaspoon fresh lemon juice
12 marshmallows	2 cups whipping cream
3/4 cup sugar	1 teaspoon vanilla

Wash and hull the berries. Place in a saucepan with marshmallows, sugar and lemon juice. Cook over low heat for 15 minutes, stirring occasionally, or until mixture is a thick syrup. Remove from heat and pass through a sieve. Cool in refrigerator. Whip the cream until stiff and blend in the berry mixture and vanilla. Pour into ice-cube trays and freeze until mushy. Beat thoroughly with a hand beater, then return mixture to the refrigerator and freeze again until firm. Cover the trays with foil until ready to serve.

Strawberry Mousse

2 cups strawberries	Dash of salt
3/4 cup sugar	1 cup whipping cream
1 tablespoon lemon juice	

Clean berries and crush with the sugar. Add the lemon juice or a couple of squirts from a "homestead lemon." Add the salt. Whip the cream until stiff. Fold the berries into the whipped cream. Place in refrigerator tray for about 2 hours, stirring once during that time.

Betty Ryan
Seattle, Washington

Strawberry Swirl

1 cup graham cracker crumbs
3 tablespoons sugar
1/4 cup melted butter or
  margarine
2 cups crushed strawberries
1 3-ounce package strawberry
  gelatin

1 cup boiling water
Water
1/2 pound marshmallows
1/2 cup milk
1 cup whipped cream or dessert
  topping

Mix graham cracker crumbs, 1 tablespoon sugar and butter and press into a 9x9-inch pan. Chill. Sprinkle remaining 2 tablespoons sugar over the berries and let stand for 30 minutes. Dissolve gelatin in boiling water. Drain the strawberries, reserving the juice. Add enough water to the juice to make 1 cup liquid, then add to gelatin and chill until partially set. Meanwhile, combine marshmallows and milk and heat until the marshmallows melt, stirring to prevent scorching. Cool thoroughly, then fold in the whipped cream. Add the berries to the gelatin, then swirl in the marshmallow-whipped cream mixture to gain a marbled effect. Pour into the crust and chill until set. Cut into squares for serving.

Thimbleberry Whip

1 quart, approximately,
  thimbleberries
Dash of salt

1/2 cup sugar
2 stiffly beaten egg whites
1 tablespoon lemon juice

Force thimbleberries through a fine sieve until you have 1 cup of puree. Heat the puree with the sugar and salt until the sugar is dissolved. Gradually pour this over the stiffly beaten egg whites, beating constantly. Add lemon juice and pile into parfait glasses. You may wish to layer the dessert with fresh whole berries with a few on the top for garnish and chill before serving.

Wild Berry Ice

2 cups hot water
2 cups sugar

2 cups wild berries
3/4 cup berry juice

Combine hot water and sugar in a saucepan; stir over heat until sugar is dissolved. Boil 5 minutes without stirring. Allow to cool. Crush berries and drain and reserve the juice. Add berries and 3/4 cup juice to the sugar syrup. Pour into freezer trays and freeze until firm. Wild raspberries or black raspberries, lowbush cranberries or blueberries may be used in this recipe. If you try cranberries, use more sugar.

Wild Berry Parfait

Vanilla ice cream
Wild strawberries or raspberries

Grated rind of 1 orange
Sugar to taste

Crush the berries slightly. Add sugar and orange rind and stir to mingle flavors. Place a layer of ice cream in the bottom of parfait glass, then a layer of prepared berries. Alternate layers of ice cream and fruit until glass is full. Freeze. When it is time to serve, drop dollop of whipped cream and a maraschino cherry on top. Other berries are excellent prepared in this fashion also. Try more than 1 kind in each glass.

Wild Strawberry Sherbet

10 ounces, approximately, frozen
  strawberries
3/4 cup sugar
2 stiffly beaten egg whites

1-1/2 teaspoons unflavored gelatin
1/2 cup water
Juice of 1 lemon

Simmer strawberries and sugar together in a saucepan for 5 to 6 minutes, stirring frequently until well blended. Soak gelatin in water for 5 minutes. Add to the hot berries and stir until gelatin is melted. Add the lemon juice. Pour into a mold and freeze until about half set. Transfer to a bowl and beat until light. Gently fold in the stiffly beaten egg whites. Return mixture to mold and freeze until firm.

MINCEMEATS

Cranberry "Mincemeat"

4 cups tart apples
1 pound chopped raisins or *dried*
  wild berries
1 cup chopped walnut meats
4 cups ground lowbush
  cranberries
1-1/2 teaspoons ground ginger
2 teaspoons salt

1/4 cup candied orange rind
1 cup lemon juice
Grated rind of 3 lemons
4 cups sugar
1-1/2 teaspoons ground cloves
1-1/2 teaspoons crystallized
  slivered ginger

Peel, core and chop apples and add to the chopped raisins or dried wild berries. Mix with remaining ingredients in a saucepan and bring to a boil over medium heat. Simmer for 5 minutes, then pack at once into hot, sterilized canning jars and seal. Process in a boiling water bath for 15 minutes. Add 4 tablespoons of melted butter to each pint of mincemeat just before you plan to use it.

Northland Mincemeat

2 pounds moose meat, cooked
  until tender
1/2 pound suet
3 pounds tart apples
2 pounds blueberries

3 pounds raisins
1 tablespoon salt
2 cups brown sugar
5 cups water or sweet cider
1 cup meat stock

Put cooked moose meat (the tough, less desirable cuts are fine here) through a food chopper and chop the suet fine. Place the meat and suet in a large preserving kettle and add the above remaining ingredients. Bring to a boil and reduce heat. Simmer slowly for 1 hour, stirring occasionally. To this mixture add the following:

2-1/2 pints blueberry or cranberry
  juice
1 teaspoon mace
1/2 teaspoon pepper
2 teaspoons allspice
2 teaspoon cloves

2 teaspoons nutmeg
2 teaspoons cinnamon
1 cup molasses
Juice and chopped peel of 1 orange
Juice and chopped peel of 1 lemon
3/4 cup vinegar

Mix all ingredients and boil for 10 minutes. Pack into sterilized canning jars, leaving 1 inch headspace. Process at 10 pounds pressure (240°F.) for 30 minutes.

Mary Taylor
Moose Pass, Alaska

Basic Red Huckleberry Sauce

1 cup red huckleberries
1/4 cup sugar
3 tablespoons cold water

2 tablespoons light corn syrup
1 tablespoon cornstarch
2 teaspoons lemon juice

Wash berries and place in a saucepan. Add sugar, 2 tablespoons cold water and syrup. Bring to a boil. Blend cornstarch and 1 tablespoon cold water, stirring gradually into berry mixture. Cook until thickened, stirring constantly. Stir in lemon juice and remove from heat. Chill. This topping is especially good on ice cream, Swedish pancakes or waffles. I like it as a topping for Cheese Pie, too.

Karen Hofstad
Petersburg, Alaska

Blueberry Sauce

1/2 cup sugar
Dash of salt
2 tablespoons cornstarch
1 cup blueberry juice

1 cup water
2 tablespoons lemon juice
3 tablespoons butter or margarine

Combine sugar, salt and cornstarch in a saucepan and mix until smooth. Add the juice and water gradually and keep stirring. Simmer over low heat until thick and clear. Remove from heat and stir in lemon juice and butter. Wonderful on waffles or blueberry hotcakes.

Crab Apple Sauce

1 quart crab apples
1/2 cup water

Sugar
Cinnamon

Stem the crab apples and rinse in lukewarm water. Drain, then place the apples in a saucepan with the 1/2 cup water. Bring to a boil and reduce heat to simmer. Cook slowly until the fruit is soft. While still warm, put through a sieve to remove seeds and skins. Add the sugar and cinnamon to suit your taste. This Crab Apple Sauce is especially good in cake, cookies and bread and can be used wherever regular applesauce is called for.

Cranberry Butter Sauce

2 cups Whole Berry Cranberry
  Sauce (see recipe, page 84)
1/4 cup butter or margarine

1/4 cup brown sugar or maple
  syrup
Cinnamon

Combine all the ingredients and heat just to the boiling point. Serve hot on waffles or pancakes.

Easiest Berry Sauce

1 cup berry juice
1 cup water

1/2 cup sugar
1 tablespoon cornstarch

Heat juice and water together. Mix sugar and cornstarch with a small amount of the liquid, then return all to the hot juice. Cook, stirring until the sauce is thick and clear. This sauce is excellent served on Berry Roll or other berry desserts.

Fruit Juice Sauce

1 cup sugar
Dash of salt
1 tablespoon cornstarch
1/2 cup boiling water

2 tablespoons lemon or orange juice
1 cup juice of blueberries, raspberries or strawberries

Mix sugar, salt and cornstarch in a saucepan and slowly add boiling water. Boil 5 minutes and then add the juices. Cool and stir in a few whole, fresh berries if available.

Glazed Cranberry Sauce

1 cup sugar
1 stick cinnamon
2 thin lemon slices

1/2 cup Port wine
1-3/4 cups lowbush cranberries

Combine first four ingredients and bring to a boil. Lower heat and simmer for 5 minutes. Add cranberries and cook gently just long enough for the skins to begin popping. Remove from heat. This gay-looking sauce for holiday ice cream can be served hot or cold.

Melba Sauce

2 cups salmonberries or raspberries
1/4 cup Wild Currant Jelly (see recipe, page 168)

Sugar
1 teaspoon cornstarch
1 tablespoon cold water

Bring the berries to a boil in a saucepan. Remove from heat and when partially cooled put through a strainer to remove seeds. Add the Wild Currant Jelly and bring to the boiling point again. Add enough sugar to suit your taste. Mix the cornstarch and cold water into a smooth paste and pour into the berry mixture. Simmer and stir until the sauce thickens slightly. Strain again. This sauce is good on ice cream, puddings and fresh fruit.

Raspberry and Wine Sauce

2 cups defrosted raspberries
1/4 cup Port wine

2 tablespoons cornstarch
Juice and grated rind of 1 orange

Place defrosted berries in a saucepan with wine. Mix cornstarch, grated orange rind and juice; add to the berries. Place over medium heat and stir until mixture becomes creamy and transparent. Cover and refrigerate for at least 24 hours before serving.
Variation: Substitute strawberries for the raspberries.

Raspberry Sauce

3 cups defrosted raspberries
Water
1/4 cup sugar
2 tablespoons cornstarch

1 tablespoon lemon juice
1/4 teaspoon almond flavoring
(optional)

Drain the juice from the defrosted raspberries and add enough water to make 1-1/2 cups liquid. Combine liquid with sugar, cornstarch and lemon juice. Cook, stirring, until mixture comes to a boil. Boil for 1 minute. One-fourth teaspoon almond flavoring may be added if desired. Serve this sauce on sundaes, over plain cake, angel cake, puddings or as a topping for cream pie.

Simple Sundae Sauce

2 cups wild strawberries

3/4 cup sugar

If needed, clean the strawberries, otherwise begin by crushing the berries just enough to get their juice flowing. In a saucepan combine the berries and sugar. Let stand for 2 hours, then bring slowly to a boil and cook for exactly 1 minute. Allow to cool. Try this over vanilla ice cream.

Tutti Frutti

No one likes to throw away good fruit during the picking seasons just because they are left over from other recipes. Here is a way to store the fruit and make a delicious sauce at the same time. As you get the extra berries, place them in a covered crock. The more types of berries the better. Include peaches or apricots, too, to equal 1/4 the total fruit. With each addition of fruit, add about half as much sugar. Add brandy or rum to suit your taste. Keep the crock in a cool, dry place — the refrigerator or the cellar work perfectly. Let the concoction stand 10 days or so after the last addition. This thick sauce makes an excellent topping.

BEVERAGES

Lowbush Cranberry Juice

Lowbush cranberries   Water

Use half as much water by volume as lowbush cranberries. Mix water and berries and boil gently for 5 minutes or a bit less. Crush and strain the mixture through a wet jelly bag to obtain a clear juice. Reserve the pulp for use in jams or desserts. Seal the juice in sterilized bottles or canning jars for later use in beverages, jellies and sauces.

Rose Hip Juice

Rose hips   Water

If possible, gather your rose hips before the first frost. Clean and remove the tails. Place the hips in a kettle with enough water to completely cover the fruit. Bring to a boil slowly, reduce the heat, and simmer for 15 minutes, or until the fruit is soft. Strain the hips through a wet jelly bag overnight. Pour the extracted juice into a container you can cover, then store it in the refrigerator, where it will keep for several weeks — ideal for having on hand throughout the preserving season.

MILK SHAKES

Finland's Berry Shake

Crushed strawberries   1-1/2 tablespoons sugar or honey
2 cups cold milk for each shake

Pour milk, sugar or honey, and strawberries into a mixing bowl. (If using frozen berries, drain off the syrup and reserve it for other use.) Beat for a minute or two with an egg beater. Pour into tall drinking glasses. Other wild berries may be used this way, too, but you may need to add more sugar for tarter berries.

Raspberry Milk Shake

1 cup raspberries   1 quart vanilla ice cream
4-1/2 cups cold milk   Mint leaves
1 cup instant nonfat milk powder

Crush the raspberries. In a large bottle combine raspberries, liquid milk and milk powder. Shake vigorously to blend well. Add ice cream and shake some more until the ingredients are thoroughly blended. Pour into tall, frosted glasses and garnish with mint leaves.

Variations: Try this basic milk shake recipe with nagoon-, straw-, or salmonberries.

Alaska Cranberry Tea

1 quart lowbush cranberries
2 cinnamon sticks
3 quarts water

6 tablespoons lemon juice
2 cups orange juice
2 cups sugar

Cook cranberries, cinnamon sticks and water until berries are tender. Strain. Add lemon, orange juice and sugar. Heat until sugar is dissolved. Serve hot.

Rachel Adkins
North Pole, Alaska

Alaska Punch

1 cup lowbush cranberries
1 cup ripe rose hips
1/2 cup water
1 cup raspberries

Dash of salt
1 cup sugar
Orange slices

Cook cranberries and rose hips in water until fruit is soft. Add raspberries and cook until they are soft, too. Drain through a wet jelly bag and squeeze to get all possible juice. Drain again to clarify the juice but do not squeeze the bag this time around. Add the sugar and salt and swirl briefly until all the sugar is dissolved. Pour over cracked ice in tall glasses. Float a thin slice of orange on top of each glass.

Cranberry Punch

1 quart Lowbush Cranberry Juice
  (see recipe, page 142)
1/2 cup sugar syrup
2 cups water

1 cup orange juice
Juice of 1/2 lemon
1 quart ginger ale or soda water

Make the sugar syrup by boiling together equal parts of sugar and water for 5 minutes. To make a quart of Lowbush Cranberry Juice, use 1 pound lowbush cranberries and 4 cups water. Mix syrup and cranberry juice with water, orange and lemon juices and chill thoroughly. Just before serving add ginger ale or soda water.

Be sure you know your berry identification. Baneberries are definitely poisonous and must be avoided — both the white and the red forms.

Huckleberry Nectar

1 quart huckleberries
1 quart water
1 cup sugar

Juice of 2 lemons
1 quart soda water

Cook the huckleberries in water until soft. Strain through a wire sieve and add sugar. Cook 5 minutes more. Strain through a cheesecloth or jelly bag. Chill thoroughly. To serve, pour the lemon juice over ice cubes in a punch bowl and add the huckleberry juice. Pour in the soda water.

Variations:
• Add a little Lowbush Cranberry Juice or orange and pineapple juice.
• Use blueberries instead of huckleberries.

Norwegian Punch

10 pounds lowbush cranberries
3 quarts water
1 ounce cream of tartar

1/2 cup hot water
Sugar

Clean and grind the cranberries. Add water and salt. Stir cream of tartar into the hot water and add to the juicy mixture. Stir well. Let stand for 2 days, stirring occasionally. Strain through a jelly bag. Measure the juice and add half as much sugar as juice. Stir well and skim if needed. Pour into sterilized bottles and cap. (This base is a good keeper.) To serve add 3 pints of water to each pint of juice. A delicious and sparkling cranberry punch.

Raspberry Punch

2 cups raspberry juice
1/4 cup sugar
1 teaspoon cornstarch
5 whole cloves

1 cinnamon stick
1 cup orange juice
3/4 cup grape juice

Boil raspberry juice and sugar together with cornstarch and spices. Cool. Add orange and grape juices and serve over cracked ice in tall glasses.

PUNCHES WITHOUT ALCOHOL

Wild Berry Vinegar for Berry Shrub

4 quarts raspberries
  or strawberries
2 quarts cider vinegar

Sugar
Mint sprigs

Clean, but do not wash, the berries. Add the vinegar to the berries in a large saucepan and allow to stand for 24 hours. Strain and measure the resulting liquid. Add 1-1/2 pounds sugar for each quart of liquid and boil gently for 30 minutes. Skim and allow to cool in the pan. When cool, pour into sterilized bottles and cap for future use in beverages.

To prepare the Berry Shrub put 3 tablespoons Berry Vinegar into iced tea glass and fill with ice and water or club soda. Garnish with a sprig of mint and serve with a straw.

PUNCHES WITH ALCOHOL

Bon Voyage Punch

2 quarts strawberries
Juice of 1 lemon
2 bottles dry white wine

2 bottles champagne
Large block of ice
Mint sprigs

Pick over and hull the strawberries; place in a bowl. Sprinkle the lemon juice over the berries and add 1 bottle of dry white wine, such as Chablis. Chill for several hours. Chill the second bottle of wine and the champagne, too. When nearly time to serve, place the ice in a large punch bowl. Combine all the liquids in the punch bowl and add a few sprigs of mint. Ladle out the punch with a strawberry in each serving.

Christmas Cordial

6 cups Lowbush Cranberry Juice
  (see recipe, page 142)
6 cups sugar

4 cups lemon-lime soda
3 cups vodka

Combine juice and sugar in a saucepan. Bring quickly to a boil and boil until syrupy — about 5 or 6 minutes. Cool to lukewarm. Stir in soda and vodka and chill in the refrigerator for a few hours before serving.

Season's Greeting Punch

1 quart Lowbush Cranberry Juice
  (see recipe, page 142)
1 quart apple juice
2 6-ounce cans frozen lemonade
  concentrate

4 12-ounce bottles ginger ale
4 cups water
1 cup vodka
6 tablespoons orange instant
  breakfast drink

Combine all ingredients and chill thoroughly. Pour over block of ice in a punch bowl for serving.

Strawberry-Wine Punch

1/2 cup water
1 cup sugar
2 cups strained orange juice
1/2 cup lemon juice

2 cups fresh strawberries
2 cups Rose wine
1 quart soda water

Cook sugar and water together to the boiling point and boil for 5 minutes. Cool slightly. Combine with orange juice, lemon juice and whole berries. Pour over ice in a punch bowl. Add wine and stir in soda water.

Hannah Weber
Quincy, Washington

WINES, LIQUEURS AND MEADS

The laws governing the making of wine for home consumption have changed considerably during the last few years. It used to be that anyone doing so was required to register with the Bureau of Alcohol, Tobacco and Firearms, but not anymore. A household with one adult is allowed to produce 100 gallons of wine per year. A household with two or more adults can legally produce a maximum of 200 gallons per year.

But you are not without some restrictions. The wine you produce must be consumed in your home. The only exception to this is if the wine is taken out of home to a wine-tasting event or contest sponsored by a formal organization. Taking your wine to a friend's home for an evening of sampling doesn't count. However, guests in your home can consume the wine you've made. Wine made for home consumption cannot be sold.

For further information regarding the making of wine for home or commercial production, contact the local office of the Bureau of Alcohol, Tobacco and Firearms.

Blueberry Wine

8 quarts blueberries
8 quarts cool water
2 quarts cane sugar

2 ounces moist yeast
1 slice toasted wholewheat bread

Mash the blueberries in a large preserving kettle. In a second kettle mix 4 quarts water and sugar; bring to a boil, boiling hard for 7 minutes. Pour syrup over berries to set their color. Add remaining 4 quarts water, stirring well. Moisten yeast with enough water to make a paste; spread yeast on the toast. Float toast, yeast side down, on surface of the kettle contents. Allow to ferment at room temperature for 2 weeks, stirring gently, but thoroughly, every 24 hours. Strain through a jelly bag, squeezing for all the liquid. Let stand another 3 days in a kettle for the sediment to settle. Siphon into sterilized bottles and cork *lightly*. When the fermentation has ceased — 3 to 4 weeks — cork bottles tightly and seal with paraffin. Store for 6 months. A year's storage time allows the wine to mellow more.

Cranberry Liqueur

3 heaping quarts lowbush
   cranberries
Fifth of Everclear

3 cups water
6 cups sugar

First day: Grind cranberries and put in stainless steel or enamel pan. Let stand 24 hours. Second day: Add Everclear and let stand 24 hours more. Third day: In separate saucepan, boil water and sugar for 5 minutes. Set aside to cool. Meanwhile strain the cranberry mixture and squeeze through cheesecloth until dry. Add sugar mixture and bottle.

Rosann Troseth
Wasilla, Alaska

Cranberry Wine

1 gallon water
1 gallon lowbush cranberries
2 pounds chopped raisins
3-1/2 pounds sugar

1 slice toasted white bread, cut
   in small squares
1 package yeast

Boil the water. Place the cranberries in a large kettle. Pour the water over the cranberries. Mash the berries daily for 6 days. Add the chopped raisins, sugar and toasted bread squares to the liquid. Stir until the sugar is dissolved. Sprinkle in the yeast. Allow to stand for 16 days. Skim and strain the liquid; pour it into sterilized bottles and seal. This wine should age between 9 and 12 months before consumption.

Marie Moke
Skagway, Alaska

Raspberry Liqueur

4 quarts red or black raspberries	7 cups sugar
4 quarts water	

Put picked-over, clean berries into a large preserving kettle and mash with a potato masher. In a separate pan bring 2 quarts water to a rapid boil and pour over the fruit to set the color. Stir well to mix, then set in a warm place. The next day dissolve the sugar in another 2 quarts water over low heat. Allow to cool to lukewarm. Then stir in the berry mixture, blending well. Set in a warm place to ferment for 2 weeks or more, stirring daily. Turn any floating berries so they will be evenly mixed. Strain through jelly bag at end of this time, squeezing the bag. Return to the kettles for 2 days to settle. Siphon off into sterilized bottles and cork *lightly*. When bubbling stops and the fermentation has ceased, cork tightly and seal with paraffin. Store for at least a year to allow the liqueur to develop flavor properly.

Wild Currant Mead

5 pounds honey	2 cups muscat raisins
4 quarts water	1 ounce moist yeast
4 quarts currants	1 slice toasted white bread

Mix honey and water in a large kettle and bring to a full boil, boiling hard for 10 minutes. Skim off all froth as it forms. Crush the currants with a potato masher. Remove the syrup from the heat and stir in the currants immediately. Allow to cool to lukewarm. Run the raisins through a fine-bladed food chopper, then add to the syrup, blending well. Moisten the yeast with enough water to make a smooth paste; spread the yeast on the toast. Place the toast, yeast side down, on top of the fruit syrup. Allow to ferment in a warm place for 2 weeks. Strain through a jelly bag, squeezing for all the juice. Return the liquid to the kettle to ferment another 2 weeks. Strain through at least four thicknesses of cheesecloth and siphon fermented liquid into sterilized bottles. Cork the bottles *lightly,* and, when the bubbling stops and all fermentation has ceased, cork them tightly and seal with paraffin. Store for 6 to 8 months before serving.

Wild Rose Hip Wine

4 pounds rose hips	1 ounce yeast
3/4 gallon water	1-1/2 pounds sugar
(1st day's use)	(7th day's use)
1-1/2 pounds sugar	1/4 gallon water
(1st day's use)	(7th day's use)

Rose hips should be ripe, red, clean and seeded. Crush or chop the hips. Place hips in a large crock and pour in 1/2 gallon boiling water. Boil 1-1/2 pounds sugar in 1 quart water for 2 minutes; allow to cool slightly. Add to the rose hip mixture. Sprinkle in the yeast. Ferment for 7 days. Strain through a jelly cloth to remove solids. Siphon the liquid into a gallon jar. Boil 1-1/2 pounds sugar in 1 quart water; allow to cool thoroughly, then add to the fermented liquid. Cover and allow fermentation to continue until finished (when the bubbling stops). Bottle and seal.

REMEDY FOR CABIN FEVER

Instead of making jam or jelly or otherwise preserving your harvest of wild berries, freeze them temporarily. Berry season is also hunting season and all the berries seem to come on at once anyhow; so don't waste time on them then. It is much simpler to freeze those that can be frozen and then make them up into jam, jelly or other such concoction during the winter when you are supposedly blessed with more time for such things. And also, making jam in January will remind you of the golden days of autumn when you were out harvesting the berries. That is one way to shorten a long winter and to combat cabin fever.

POTPOURRI

Berrylets

Blueberries or raspberries,
   enough to make 2 cups pulp
4 cups sugar
4 envelopes unflavored gelatin

1 cup cold water
1/2 teaspoon almond flavoring
1 cup chopped walnuts
Powdered sugar

Crush berries and put through a sieve. Add sugar to pulp. Soak gelatin in the water for 5 minutes. Add to berry mixture and cook for 20 minutes, stirring with a wooden spoon to prevent sticking. Remove from heat. Add almond flavoring and chopped nuts. Pour into a greased cake pan. Let stand 2 days or until stiff and firm. Cut into squares and roll each square in powdered sugar. Store in cool, dry place.

Virginia Culver
Chugiak, Alaska

Berry Spoon Loaf

3 cups sugar
1-1/2 cups milk
1/2 teaspoon salt

2 tablespoons butter or margarine
1 cup chopped nuts
1 cup *dried* serviceberries

Combine sugar, milk, salt and butter in a large saucepan. Bring to a boil and boil until a little of the syrup dropped in a cup of cold water will form a soft ball. Be sure to cook it enough. Stir in the nuts and dried berries. Cook slowly until the mass of candy begins to form a large lump in the pan, stirring constantly to avoid scorching. Wring out a clean tea towel in cold water. Remove the candy to one end of the tea towel, forming a long roll. Roll up in the towel and wrap a dry towel around it. When the candy is set, unwrap it and slice the roll into 1/2-inch-thick pieces. Allow to dry, then store the candy in an airtight container.

Variation: If you don't have enough dried serviceberries, add some chopped dates instead.

Blueberry Coconuts

1 cup shredded coconut
2 tablespoons butter or margarine
1 small egg
Dash of salt

1 teaspoon vanilla
1/2 teaspoon nutmeg
Powdered sugar
1/2 cup blueberry puree

Toast coconut in the oven until it turns a light brown. Soften the butter in a bowl and stir in unbeaten egg, salt, vanilla and nutmeg. Gradually stir in 1/2 cup powdered sugar. Add the puree and another 1/2 cup powdered sugar and beat thoroughly. Add the coconut (leaving a little to use later) and enough more powdered sugar to make the candy as stiff as possible. Transfer the mass to a large sheet of waxed paper sprinkled liberally with powdered sugar. Knead the candy as you would bread dough, adding more sugar if necessary. Pinch off small bits of the candy and roll between your palms to form balls the size of large marbles. Place the balls on a clean sheet of waxed paper and sprinkle the remaining coconut on top each. Press the center down with your thumb. After the surface of the candy dries, turn the balls over to dry the other side. Store in an airtight container with waxed paper between the layers.

Candied Rose Hips

1-1/2 cups ripe rose hips   1/4 cup water
1/2 cup sugar   Additional sugar

Remove seeds from rose hips with the sharp tip of a knife. Mix the 1/2 cup sugar with water and boil briefly to make a syrup. Add rose hips and boil gently 10 to 12 minutes or until the fruit is soft. Lift hips from the syrup with a skimmer and set to drain on waxed paper. While hips are still moist, dust them with sugar. If possible, dry the hips slowly in the sun; if not possible, dry them in an oven set at its lowest temperature, being sure to leave the oven door ajar so moisture can escape. Add more sugar if the candy is sticky. Store the candied hips in an airtight metal container with waxed paper between the layers. Candied Rose Hips can be used with, or in place of, nuts and raisins in cookies and in puddings with grated lemon rind and upside down cakes, or as snacks.

Cranberry Wafers

2 cups sugar   1/4 cup Lowbush Cranberry Juice
1/4 cup water   (see recipe, page 142)
1 teaspoon lemon or
   "homestead lemon" juice

Mix sugar, water and juices in a saucepan and boil, without stirring, until a little dropped in cold water forms a firm ball. Remove from heat and set saucepan in a pan of cold water. Beat until the mixture appears cloudy. Drop by teaspoonfuls onto waxed paper to form wafers or patties.

Our kids need something besides, or in place of, candy bars and potato chips. Be a wise mother and make your family a treat. Make them some Fruit Leather. Fruit leather is not as tough as it sounds. It is a slightly tart, nutritious snack made from fresh or dried fruits. It is easily made in the oven or outside in the sun.
Mary Alice Griffis
Nome Nugget

Fruit Squares

1 cup sugar	2-1/2 cups puffed rice cereal
2 beaten eggs	3/4 cup chopped almonds
1/4 teaspoon salt	1 teaspoon vanilla
1 cup chopped *dried* berries	Toasted coconut
2 cups finely chopped, shredded coconut	

Mix sugar, eggs and salt; blend in the dried berries and shredded coconut. Pour into a skillet and cook slowly 10 to 15 minutes, stirring constantly. Remove from heat and add the cereal, nuts and vanilla, mixing well. Let stand for 15 minutes. Spread in a pan and with a very sharp knife cut 1-inch squares and dredge each square in toasted coconut.

Wild Berry Patties

1 egg yolk	1/4 cup Lowbush Cranberry Juice
Grated orange peel to taste	(see recipe, page 142)
2 tablespoons butter or margarine	Powdered sugar

Mix egg yolk, orange peel (dried orange peel is even better than fresh) and butter. Add the cranberry juice. Now gradually stir in the powdered sugar until you can stir no more. Place on a surface covered with powdered sugar. Knead the candy, working in as much of the powdered sugar as it will accept. Pinch off small bits of the candy, rolling into balls. Place an inch apart on waxed paper. Press your thumb into the center of each ball to make a hollow patty. Let the patties stand overnight to dry; turn the patties over to dry the other side.

Blueberry Syrup

4 cups blueberry juice	1 to 2 cups corn syrup
2 cups sugar	

Place ingredients in a saucepan and bring to a boil. Boil for about 3 minutes. The corn syrup will thicken the juice without making it excessively sweet. Seal in hot, sterilized canning jars or keep frozen. This is good on ice cream, hotcakes or in beverages. Also good as a sauce for puddings.

Martha Wilson
Toledo, Oregon

Cranberry Syrup

2 pounds lowbush cranberries	2 cups sugar
1 cup water	1/2 cup orange juice

Clean berries and add them to the water in a saucepan. Cook over medium heat until berries soften. Crush with a potato masher and continue cooking slowly another 10 minutes. Drain overnight in a dampened jelly bag, without squeezing. The pulp may be saved for other use. Add the sugar to the juice and bring to a boil and boil slowly for 5 minutes. Add the orange juice and boil 1 minute more. You may wish to add more sugar. Pour into sterilized canning jars or bottles and seal. This syrup can be used in a variety of ways.

Crowberry Syrup

Crowberries to make 1 quart juice	Juice of 1 lemon
1 pint water	1/2 teaspoon cinnamon
1-1/2 cups sugar	1 tablespoon butter

Crush berries and cook in water until soft. Strain overnight through a moist jelly bag. Combine with other ingredients and bring to a boil quickly. Boil for 3 minutes. Bottle and seal immediately, using sterilized bottles or canning jars.

Mixed Berry Syrup

Berries and/or berry juices	Sugar

During the preserving season save all your odds and ends of berries and berry juices and put them in a covered container in the refrigerator. When you accumulate enough to make a respectable batch of syrup (4 or 5 cups) put them in a saucepan and bring to a boil. Reduce the heat and simmer for 5 minutes. Strain through a moistened jelly bag overnight, but don't squeeze the bag. Add 3/4 cup sugar to each 2 cups juice and bring to a boil. Reduce heat to simmer and cook slowly 5 to 10 minutes. This makes a delicious syrup with many uses. If you wish a heavier syrup, simply add more sugar.

Raspberry Syrup

3 cups wild raspberries   Sugar
1/2 cup water

Sort and clean raspberries and simmer in water for 5 minutes. Place fruit in a damp jelly bag and strain overnight; do not squeeze the bag. Put the pulp through a sieve and use for raspberry puree in making jam or other dishes. Pour the juice into a saucepan and stir in sugar (1/4 cup sugar for each cup juice). Bring to a slow boil, then reduce heat and simmer for 10 minutes. An excellent sweetener for beverages and good, too, as a sauce for hotcakes.

Red Huckleberry Syrup

Red huckleberries   Sugar
Water   Dash of salt

Cook berries in a small amount of water. Place the softened berries in a jelly bag and drain overnight; do not squeeze bag or syrup will be cloudy. Add 2 cups sugar to each quart of juice. Add a dash of salt. Cook over low heat until the berry liquid becomes syrupy. It thickens as it cools. Pour into sterilized canning jars and seal or keep refrigerated. It is delicious on sundaes, hotcakes and waffles.

Rose Hip Syrup

4 cups rose hips   2 cups sugar
2 cups water

Clean and remove tails and stems of rose hips and wash thoroughly. Measure water and rose hips into a saucepan. Boil for 20 minutes on low heat. Strain through a jelly bag or cheesecloth to remove sediment. Return the juice to the pan and add the sugar. Boil again for 5 minutes. Store in the refrigerator where it will keep almost indefinitely. This is especially good in combination with other juices or syrups because of its high Vitamin C content. The pulp may be saved and used with other fruit for jam.

University of Alaska
Cooperative Extension Service

Fruit Leather

2 cups your choice crushed berries

3 tablespoons sugar

Mix berries with sugar. (Too much sugar makes a brittle leather.) Bring to a rolling boil. Reduce to medium heat and stir constantly until syrupy. Put through a sieve to remove seeds; allow to cool slightly. Pour 6-inch-wide by 1/4-inch-thick strips down the length of a slightly greased cookie sheet. Dry in an oven set between 140° and 150°, leaving the oven door ajar to allow moisture to escape. When the puree is firm to the touch — 5 to 6 hours time — try to peel the Fruit Leather off the pan. *If it adheres to the cookie sheet, it's not ready to be removed!* Roll up the leather in plastic wrap for storage. It keeps about a month in the open, and longer in the freezer. You can also dry the fruit in the sun — 20 to 24 hours — but cover it to keep the bugs away.

Nagoonberry Hardtack

4 cups nagoonberries
1 cup shredded coconut
1 cup rolled oats

1/4 cup sugar
2 cups flour

Preheat oven to 250°. Mash berries thoroughly in a bowl. Mix in coconut and rolled oats, then the sugar. Stir in flour until dough is firm. Drop by spoonfuls onto an oiled cookie sheet. Flatten each mound with the bottom of a glass. Bake until hard. The end product is a semi-sweet cookie.

Variations:
• Substitute an equal amount of honey for sugar.
• Substitute an equal amount of cornmeal for flour.

Karen Jettmar
Gustavus, Alaska

Pemmican "C"

1 pound dried game meat
1 pound animal fat
1/2 cup *dried* rose hips

1 cup *dried* serviceberries, blueberries or crowberries

Cut fat into small pieces and cook in a skillet until rendered. Discard any remaining lumps. Pour the liquid fat over the dried meat, then add dried berries and rose hips. Set aside until fat has congealed. Place on a large board and pound with a wooden mallet until the mixture is reduced to a pulpy mass about the consistency of hamburger. Shape this into small bars; roll up each bar in plastic wrap. Place the bars in plastic bags, several to a bag, and store in a cool, dry place, or freeze until needed. This sustaining trail food is rich in Vitamin C.

Akutaq

1 cup shortening or lard
1/2 cup seal oil (if seal oil is not available, use corn oil)
1/4 to 1/2 cup sugar depending on taste

2-1/2 to 3 cups boned fish, boiled and squeezed dry
4 cups wild berries

Put shortening into large bowl. Squeeze and flatten with the hands until smooth and soft; then add oil to make it even smoother. Mix and blend with hands until soft enough. Add sugar and mix well. Then add the fish, crumbling it as you add it and sort of scatter it in little by little until all the fish is in the mixture. At this point the akutaq should be puffed up, sort of like whipped cream. Next add the berries as you did the fish. After all is done, freeze until firm. More sugar may be added when served. Most Eskimos have the ingredients for akutaq readily available.

Indian Ice Cream

The Indians of British Columbia, the Yukon and Alaska mix the soopalallie berries with sugar and water and beat the mixture with their hands. It looks a bit like whipped cream and is a favorite dish among northern Indians. The raw berry is very bitter due to the presence of saponin. Another common name for this fruit is Soapberry.

Karen Clark
Cassiar, British Columbia

Our Favorite Eskimo Ice Cream

1 to 1-1/2 quarts berries
1/2 to 3/4 cup shortening

Sugar

We use salmonberries, blueberries or blackberries. Cream shortening and sugar until fluffy. You can add a little of the berry juice to make this softer if you wish. Add berries, a small amount at a time, until you use them all up. Serve with smoked salmon strips.

Audrey Rearden
Homer, Alaska

Tiyulik (Berries with Fish Liver)

12 trout livers (or 6 salmon livers)

2-1/2 quarts crowberries or other berries

Clean the livers thoroughly and put to boil with a little water for 10 minutes. Remove from heat and cool. Mash the livers with a fork and add a little of the broth to make of a smooth consistency. Add the berries and mix well. Rich in vitamins A, D and C and iron.

PRESERVES

Testing Fruit Juice for Pectin

If you are stuck wondering if the berries you have picked have enough natural pectin to jell, test their juice by either of these 2 simple methods provided by Robbie Jayne Johnson of Anchorage, Alaska:

Method I: To 1 teaspoon of cooked juice, add 1 teaspoon of grain alcohol and stir slowly. You can discover the berries' natural jelling ability by keeping in mind that

   a. juices rich in pectin will form a large amount of bulky, gelatinous material.
   b. juices moderately rich in pectin will form a few pieces of gelatinous material.
   c. juices poor in pectin will form small, flaky pieces of sediment.

Method II: Mix 2 teaspoons sugar, 1 tablespoon Epsom salts and 2 tablespoons cooked juice. Stir well and let stand for 20 minutes. If the mixture forms a semi-solid mass, the juice contains sufficient pectin to jell.

The Sheet Test for Jelly

If you do not have a jelly thermometer to tell you when the boiling juice has reached the jelly stage, use the "sheet" test instead. Dip a cold, metal spoon into the boiling liquid and then hold it from 12 to 18 inches above the pan but out of the path of rising steam. Turn the spoon so the jelly runs off the edge. If 2 or more drops form and run together before dripping off the edge of the spoon as separate drops, the jelly stage has been reached. It usually takes from 8 to 15 minutes to reach the sheet or jelly stage.

Another berry cleaning method is to set up an electric fan out of doors. Slowly pour the berries from above the fan so they fall through the moving air to a large container below. Leaves and trash will be blown away.

Apple-Mountain Ash Jelly

4 pounds mountain ash berries
4 pounds tart apples, quartered
  and cored

Water
Sugar

Bring the berries and apples to a boil in separate containers with just enough water to cover them. Allow them to simmer until soft. Strain them separately through a damp jelly bag. Measure equal parts of each juice into large saucepan. Add 1 cup sugar to each cup of the mixture; add a sprig of mint, too, if available. Boil the juice to the jelly stage, which should take about 10 minutes. Pour the jelly into hot sterilized jelly glasses and seal with paraffin and lids.

Blueberry Jelly

Ripe blueberries
Underripe blueberries

Water
Sugar

Use half ripe blueberries and half slightly green blueberries for a better flavor. Simmer the berries with just enough water to keep from scorching. Strain overnight through a moistened jelly bag or several layers of cheesecloth. Do not squeeze. Measure the juice and add equal parts of sugar. Heat on low heat for 3 minutes, stirring. Pour into hot, sterilized jelly glasses and allow to set until cool. Seal with paraffin and lids.

Crab Apple Jelly

Crab apples to make 4 cups
  of juice (about 2-1/2 to 3
  pounds)

Water
3 cups sugar
1/4 teaspoon cinnamon (optional)

Wash and stem wild crab apples and put in a large saucepan with water enough to cover fruit completely. Simmer until apples are soft. Extract juice by draining through a damp jelly bag overnight. Return juice to pan and add sugar and cinnamon. Boil rapidly until juice reaches the jelly stage. Skim off foam, if any forms, and pour into hot, sterilized jelly glasses. Seal immediately with paraffin and lids. Crab apples are good combined with almost any of our berries which will help to stretch the yield if you are short on quantity.

Overripe berries should never be used in canning.
Use them, instead, in jams or fruit butters.

Cranberry Jelly

2 quarts lowbush cranberries   5 cups sugar
4 cups water

Cook cranberries in boiling water for 5 minutes. Strain berries through a moist jelly bag, squeezing from time to time to extract as much juice as possible. Allow juice to settle for an hour or so and again strain through the jelly bag, without squeezing this time, to ensure a clear jelly. Add the sugar and bring to a boil. Remove from heat at once, ladle into hot, sterilized jelly glasses and seal with paraffin and lids.
Variations: Spiced Cranberry Jelly. Add a 2-inch cinnamon stick, 24 whole cloves and 6 whole allspice during the initial berry cooking. Cranberry Jelly with Celery. Fold in 1-1/2 cups chopped celery to the jelly as it begins to thicken.

Highbush Cranberry Jelly

4 cups highbush cranberries   Sugar
3 cups water

Simmer berries and water to stimulate juice extraction, then boil rapidly for 5 minutes. Strain through damp jelly bag or several layers of cheesecloth. Measure the juice into pan and add 2/3 cup sugar for each cup of juice. Bring to a boil and stir until the jelly stage is reached. Pour into hot, sterilized jelly glasses and seal with paraffin and lids.

University of Alaska
Cooperative Extension Service

Lowbush Cranberry Jelly

1 quart lowbush cranberries   3 cups sugar
2-1/2 cups water   3 ounces liquid pectin

Boil berries and water together and strain through jelly bag, squeezing hard. Let settle and strain again (without squeezing this time) to ensure a clear jelly. You should have about 3 cups of juice. Add sugar and pectin, following directions on package. Pour into hot, sterilized jelly glasses and seal with paraffin and lids. Store in cool place.

University of Alaska
Cooperative Extension Service

Strawberries lack pectin, even when ripe, so proceed accordingly.

Mountain Ash Jelly

Mountain ash berries   Sugar
Water

Use fully ripe mountain ash berries; remove stems and boil with a little water until the fruit is soft. Crush the hot berries and drain through a damp jelly bag without squeezing. Measure the juice into a large saucepan, add 1 cup of sugar for each cup of juice and stir. Bring to a boil and boil until the jelly stage is reached. Skim off any foam and pour into hot, sterilized jars and seal with paraffin and lids. This jelly has a bittersweet taste and is particularly good served with meat dishes.

Red Huckleberry Jelly

Red huckleberries to make 4 cups   3 cups sugar
   juice

Prepare the juice by boiling crushed berries with just enough water to keep them from sticking. Squeeze through a jelly bag. Clean the bag and place pulp and juice in it again. This time do not squeeze the bag, allowing the juice to drain naturally and slowly. Measure 4 cups juice into a saucepan and boil for 5 minutes. Add sugar and boil rapidly until the mixture will jell when dribbled from a spoon. Skim off the foam. Remove from heat, pour into hot, sterilized jelly glasses and seal with paraffin and lids.

Rose Hip Jelly

2 cups cleaned and seeded   4 tablespoons lemon juice
   rose hips   Sugar
2 cups water

Place rose hips in a pan with the water. Boil until the hips are soft. Put through a coarse sieve and drain through a jelly bag. Measure the juice into saucepan and add the lemon juice. Add 3/4 as much sugar as you have juice. Boil rapidly for 10 minutes and test for the jelly stage. If the test is negative, continue cooking the juice until it jells. Pour into hot, sterilized jelly glasses and seal at once with paraffin and lids.

The University of Alaska Cooperative Extension Service recommends
freezing wild berries before extracting the juice for jelly making.
Freezing prior to extracting yields a greater volume of juice.

Salmonberry or Cloudberry Jelly

Salmonberries or
  cloudberries to
  make 4 cups juice
	1/4 cup water
	3 cups sugar
	A few drops lemon juice

The easy way to procure juice for these or other berries is to use the pressure cooker. Crush sorted fruit and add about 1/4 cup water. Put the cover on the cooker and bring the pressure up to 15 pounds. Remove from heat and allow the pressure to drop to normal. Strain through a fine sieve. Measure 4 cups juice into a large saucepan and add the sugar and lemon juice. Cook to the jelly stage, testing after the first 5 minutes of rapid boiling. Skim off the foam and pour quickly into hot, sterilized jelly glasses. Seal with paraffin and lids.

Wild Currant Jelly

Currants to make 4 cups juice Water	3 cups sugar

Clean currants and remove leaves and other debris. Leave the stems on the fruit. Cook in a large, flat-bottomed saucepan slowly with a small amount of water. Simmer until soft. Crush and strain through a damp jelly bag. Do not squeeze the bag. Return juice to the pan and bring to a rapid boil for 3 minutes. Add the sugar. Stir until sugar is completely dissolved, then bring to a boil again. Test for jelly stage after 3 minutes. Skim off foam, pour into hot, sterilized jelly glasses. Seal with paraffin and lids.

Wineberry (Nagoonberry) Jelly

3 cups wineberry (nagoonberry) juice	Water 1-1/4 cups sugar

For this recipe, the sugar must be warmed in an oven at a low temperature so that it will dissolve quickly when added to the juice. Carefully clean berries (do not rinse water over this delicate fruit) and prepare juice by cooking for 3 minutes with only enough water to keep the fruit from burning. Drain juice through a jelly bag. *Do not* squeeze the bag or jelly will be cloudy. Measure juice into a saucepan and boil for 5 minutes. Add the warm sugar. Continue boiling rapidly until the juice has reached the jelly stage, continually skimming off foam. Test for jelly after 5 minutes. Once the jelly sheets, pour into hot, sterilized, jelly glasses. Seal with paraffin and lids.

Cranberry Luscious

2 cups currants	2 cups raspberries
4 cups lowbush cranberries	2 cups blueberries
2 cups strawberries	Sugar

Clean the currants, but don't remove the stems. Clean and stem the other berries. Place currants into kettle and crush enough to start the juice. Cook the currants, stirring and mashing all the while, until they appear whitish. Strain through a jelly bag and add 1 cup sugar for each cup juice to make currant syrup. In a separate container combine all uncooked berries and weigh. Add as much sugar as there is uncooked fruit by weight. Pour currant syrup over the fresh fruit mixture and let stand overnight. Next day bring the mixture to boil for 15 minutes, then set it aside in a cool place for 48 hours, allowing the berries to absorb the syrup and become plump. Heat again, then pour into hot, sterilized canning jars and seal with lids. Process for 15 minutes in a boiling water bath.

Cranbutter

6 cups highbush cranberry puree	1-1/2 teaspoons allspice
4 cups granulated sugar	1/2 teaspoon nutmeg
1 tablespoon cinnamon	

Put cranberry puree in a large saucepan and add the remaining ingredients. Cook for 30 minutes over medium heat, stirring frequently. Pour into sterilized jars and seal immediately. When preparing highbush cranberries to make jelly, I press the cooked berries through a sieve. The resulting juice is cloudy and I strain it through a cloth. What is retained in the cloth is a smooth cranberry puree suitable to make into cranbutter.

Maureen Wright
May Creek, Alaska

When making jelly or jam it is well to use a large kettle because the liquid increases greatly in bulk as it boils. It may boil over and create an unholy mess if the saucepan is too small.

Lowbush Cranberry Marmalade

2 oranges	4 cups lowbush cranberries
1 lemon	6-1/2 cups sugar
1/8 teaspoon baking soda	3 ounces liquid pectin
1-3/4 cups water	

Remove seeds from the oranges and lemon and cut fruit into large pieces. Do not remove peels. Grind fruit. Add the baking soda and water; cover and simmer for 20 minutes, stirring occasionally. Add berries and continue simmering, covered, for another 10 minutes. Measure exactly 5 cups of the prepared fruit into a large saucepan and add the sugar. Bring to a full, rolling boil for 1 minute. Remove from heat and stir in the pectin at once. Skim and stir for about 5 minutes, allowing the marmalade to cool slightly. Ladle into hot, sterilized, canning jars and seal with lids. Process for 15 minutes in a boiling water bath.

Raspberry-Currant Preserves

2 pounds red currants	4 pounds raspberries
Water	Sugar

Wash the currants and cook for 15 minutes in enough water to prevent the berries from scorching. Drain through a damp jelly bag for juice. Wash the raspberries, but only if really necessary, and place them in a large saucepan. Pour the currant juice over the raspberries and gently heat for 5 minutes. Measure the fruit mixture and add 1 cup sugar for each 2 cups fruit. Cook mixture about 10 minutes or until it jells and sheets from a metal spoon. Stir as carefully as possible so the berries will not be crushed. Pour into hot, sterilized canning jars and seal with lids. Process in a boiling water bath for 15 minutes.

Hannah Weber
Quincy, Washington

Rose Hip Butter

Rose hips	Cinnamon stick
Sugar	5 or 6 whole cloves

Pick rose hips after the first frost while they are still red but ripe. Prepare the butter the same day the hips are picked, if possible. Simmer hips until softened. Remove seeds and skins by pressing through a sieve. By volume, add half as much sugar as you have pulp. Put the pulp in a saucepan and add the cinnamon stick and whole cloves. Heat slowly, covered, until all the sugar is dissolved. Then uncover and cook slowly until the butter is thick, stirring constantly to prevent sticking. Pack in hot, sterilized canning jars and seal with lids at once. Process 15 minutes in a boiling water bath.

Karen Clark
Cassiar, British Columbia

Salmonberry Preserves

Salmonberries   Sugar

Combine equal amounts of salmonberries and sugar and cook the mixture slowly for 15 minutes. Remove from heat. Remove berries to a separate dish with a slotted spoon. Boil remaining juice hard for 15 minutes, then remove from heat. Stir the berries back into the juice. Spoon the preserves into hot, sterilized, canning jars and seal with lids. Process for 15 minutes in a boiling water bath.

University of Alaska
Cooperative Extension Service

Spiced Currants

1-1/2 pounds currants   1 teaspoon cinnamon
1 pound brown sugar   1 teaspoon cloves
1 cup mild cider vinegar   1 teaspoon allspice (optional)

Wash the currants, removing stems. Place in a saucepan, add the remaining ingredients and heat to the boiling point. Reduce heat and simmer slowly for 1 hour, stirring to prevent sticking. Pour into hot, sterilized canning jars and seal with lids. Process for 15 minutes in a boiling water bath.

Strawberry Conserve

3 pints wild strawberries   1/2 pound seedless raisins
2 cups fresh, chopped pineapple 1 orange
Juice of 1 lemon   Sugar
1/2 cup chopped walnuts

Clean and slightly crush the berries. Put pineapple through a food chopper and measure. Grind raisins and orange (including rind), add lemon juice and combine all fruits. Measure the mixture and, for each cup of fruit, add 1 cup sugar. Cook until thick, stirring often. Add nuts after 10 minutes of cooking. Pour into hot, sterilized jars and seal with lids. Process 15 minutes in a boiling water bath. This is a good way to stretch a few wild strawberries.

Strawberry Preserves Deluxe

4 cups wild strawberries   4 tablespoons lemon juice
5 cups sugar

Mix the berries and sugar and let stand for several hours or overnight. Then place over extremely low heat until simmering. Add the lemon juice and boil rapidly for 10 minutes or until mixture is clear and thick. Let stand overnight. Pack cold into hot, sterilized canning jars and seal with lids. Process for 15 minutes in a boiling water bath.

University of Alaska
Cooperative Extension Service

Sunkissed Strawberry Preserves

Strawberries   Sugar

Do not wash strawberries. Crush berries and gently stir in an equal amount of sugar by volume. Pour onto large platters in a thin layer. (Several platters may be necessary.) *Do not use metal containers.* Place a clean sheet of glass over each platter and set outdoors in the sunlight. Bring indoors at night and set out again the next morning when the sun is warm. It will take about three days of good sunlight to "cook" the preserves. Take samples after the first day to tell when the berries are thoroughly cooked. Pack in hot, sterilized, canning jars, seal with lids and store in a cool place. This is the "best ever" way of preserving strawberries.

Wild Currant Preserves

3 pounds wild currants   3 pounds sugar

Clean and sort currants. Cook slowly until the juice flows freely. Add sugar and then boil the mixture rapidly for 20 minutes. Pour into hot, sterilized, canning jars and seal with lids. Process for 15 minutes in a boiling water bath.

Wild Strawberry-Pineapple Conserve

2 cups strawberries   2 cups sugar
2 cups canned, crushed pineapple   1 cup chopped pecans

Mix the strawberries, pineapple and sugar and let stand overnight. Simmer the mixture slowly to develop the juice. Then boil rapidly for 10 minutes, stirring constantly. Remove from heat. Add the nuts. Ladle into hot, sterilized, canning jars and seal with lids. Process for 15 minutes in a boiling water bath.

University of Alaska
Cooperative Extension Service

CANNING BERRIES

Canning in General

Wild berries may be safely processed using the water bath method. If you have a pressure canner it would be well to have the pressure gauge checked before starting your canning season. These gauges can sometimes be off several pounds. Be sure all your canning equipment is thoroughly cleaned. Even though equipment was clean when it was put away the last time you used it, it does accumulate dirt even in storage.

Any large metal container should serve well for a boiling-water bath canner. In days long gone by we used to use an old-fashioned copper wash boiler for a canner. We fitted it with a homemade wooden rack. Check all glass jars and lids and discard any imperfect ones such as those dented, cracked or chipped. Imperfections can cause imperfect sealing and thus cause spoilage of the fruit. Glass jars must be washed in hot, soapy water and well rinsed before using, even if they were put away clean after their last use. Wash them just before using. Likewise, wash and rinse all lids. Heat the clean jars and lids in clean water before packing with hot fruit. Be sure to follow manufacturer's instructions implicitly. Rubber rings, if used, should be clean and new.

Tin cans and lids must be in perfect condition. Discard any dented, bent or rusty cans and lids with damaged gaskets. Just before using, wash cans in clean water and turn upside down to drain. Washing lids may damage the gaskets, so they should be left in paper wrapping until the last minute when they may be wiped with a damp cloth.

Test the can sealer before using. To do this put a little water into a test can, seal it and dunk in boiling water for a few seconds. If bubbles rise from the can, the seal is not tight. Follow the manufacturer's directions to adjust the sealer.

Always select fresh, firm berries for canning and can quickly as they tend to lose their freshness rapidly. Wash the berries if needed. This should not be necessary with fruit gathered away from dusty places. However, dirt often contains harmful bacteria, so if in doubt, wash. Don't allow the berries to soak but rinse them quickly in several changes of water. Always handle the fruit gently to avoid bruising.

Berries may be raw packed or hot packed (preheated and packed hot). Raw fruit needs to be packed in quite tightly because processing will cause it to shrink. Hot berries should be at, or near, boiling point when packed and may be packed more loosely.

There should be enough liquid (syrup, juice or water) to fill in the space around the berries and to completely cover them. To remove air bubbles from filled jars, simply slide a table knife blade down the sides in several places. Then add more liquid if needed to cover the fruit, but leave a little headspace at the top. Be sure to wipe rims of jars before putting on sealing lids. Some juice my have been spilled during the filling. Follow manufacturer's directions exactly.

Tin cans must be "exhausted" before sealing raw fruit. Hot fruit may be sealed if you are sure the temperature has not gone below 170°. To make sure, test with a thermometer, thrusting the bulb into the center of the can. To exhaust, place filled, open cans on a rack in a kettle in which there is enough boiling water to come about 2 inches below the can tops. Cover the kettle and bring the water to boiling. Boil until the thermometer inserted in the middle of a can registers 170°. Remove the cans from the boiling water 1 at a time and add boiling packing liquid as needed to give the correct headspace. Put clean lids on the cans and seal at once.

Complete sealing of glass jars is necessary as they are taken from the hot water bath. If some liquid boiled away during processing, *do not open jar to add more.* Seal it just as it is. Cool with top side up, on folded cloth or rack; never set on cold surface and do not allow drafts to reach hot jars. However, never slow the cooling by covering the jars.

Tin cans should be immediately immersed in cold water to cool them. Change the water as needed for rapid cooling. Remove cans from water when they are still slightly warm and finish cooling and drying in the air. Air should be able to reach all cans so it is well to stagger them in the stack until they are completely cooled.

The next day test the seal on each canning jar by turning the jar partly over in your hands. If you find a leaky jar use the contents at once. Before storing canned berries wipe the entire container with a damp cloth to remove any spilled fruit or juice. Label to show contents and date. Canned fruit should be stored in a cool, dry place.

Processing in Boiling Water Bath

Put filled glass jars or tin cans into canning vessel of hot or boiling water. For raw pack in glass, have water in canner hot but not boiling. For all other types of pack use boiling water.

Add boiling water if needed to bring water an inch or so over tops of containers. Be careful not to pour the boiling water directly on to the glass jars. Cover the canning vessel.

When water in canner comes to a full rolling boil start to count the number of minutes needed for processing. Boil gently and continuously for recommended time. Remove containers immediately when processing time is up.

One minute additional boiling time is needed for each 1,000 feet above sea level. At 1,000 feet add 1 minute to processing time. At 2,000 feet add 2 minutes and at 3,000 feet add 3 minutes. Four minutes is right for 4,000 feet elevation.

To can berries with the raw pack method clean and drain the fruit. Fill glass jars within 1/2 inch of top, shaking berries down as you fill the jars. Cover with boiling syrup, leaving 1/2 inch head space at the top. Adjust lids and process in boiling water bath. Pint jars should be processed for 10 minutes and quarts for 15 minutes. Complete the seal as soon as jars are removed from canner if they are not of the self sealing type. In tin cans, fill to 1/4 inch from top, shaking down the berries as you fill the cans. Fill to the top with boiling syrup. Exhaust to 170° for 10 minutes and seal the cans. Process in boiling water bath for 15 minutes for No. 2 cans or 15 minutes for No. 2-1/2 cans.

To can berries with the hot pack method be sure to use firm berries. Clean and drain if necessary. Add 1/2 cup sugar to each quart of berries. Cover saucepan and bring to a boil, shaking pan to keep fruit from sticking. Pack hot berries in glass jars to 1/2 inch from top and adjust the jar lids. Process in boiling water bath 10 minutes for pints and 15 minutes for quarts. Complete seal as soon as jars are removed from the canner if closures are not selfsealing. In tin cans you will need to pack the hot berries to the top. Exhaust for 10 minutes at 170°. Seal cans and process in boiling water bath. Process No. 2 cans for 15 minutes and No. 2-1/2 cans for 20 minutes.

To can berry juice heat the juice to simmering. Strain through a wet jelly bag or other cloth. If sweet juice is desired add from 1 to 1-1/2 cups of sugar to each gallon of juice. Fill glass jars to almost the top with the hot juice. Adjust lids and process in boiling water bath for 5 minutes for either pints or quarts. Remove jars from canner and complete the seal. If you are using tin cans, fill to the top with the hot juice and seal at once. Process in the boiling water bath for 5 minutes for both No. 2 and No. 2-1/2 cans.

For canning berry purees simmer crushed fruit with a little water to keep from sticking. If the fruit is juicy, it may not be necessary to add any water but stir the pulp frequently to prevent sticking in any case. Put through a strainer or food mill and add sugar to taste. Heat again to the simmer point. Pack while still hot in glass jars to within 1/2 inch of the top. Adjust lids and process in boiling water bath for 10 minutes for either pint or quart jars. Complete seals, if necessary, as soon as jars are removed from water. Or, pack to the top in tin cans and exhaust at 170° for 10 minutes and seal cans. Process in boiling water bath for 10 minutes for either pints or quarts.

Sweetening Berries

Sweetening helps canned berries hold their shape and retain the natural color and flavor. Very juicy berries, packed hot, can have sugar added without adding liquid. Sugar syrup may be used for many berries. Use the type of syrup that suits your taste.

Bring required amounts of sugar and water to a boil and boil gently for 5 minutes. Use as a canning or freezing syrup or as sweetener for beverages.

Type of Syrup	Sugar	Water	Yield
Thin syrup	1 cup	2 cups	2-1/2 cups
Medium thin	1 cup	1-1/2 cups	2 cups
Medium	1 cup	1 cup	1-1/2 cups
Heavy	1 cup	3/4 cup	1-1/4

Recipe may be doubled or tripled as needed. Yield is approximate. Fruit juice may be substituted for water if desired.

Sugar Added Directly to Berries

For juicy fruit to be hot packed, add 1/2 cup sugar to each quart of raw berries. Heat to simmering over low heat. Pack berries in the containers and pour the juice over them, leaving headspace.

Sweeteners without Sugar

Light corn syrup or mild flavored honey can be used to replace half of the sugar called for. Do not use brown sugar, sorghum or molasses. Granulated sugar replacement can be used if you wish; use 1/2 cup of the replacement to 4 cups of water. Bring to a boil and boil gently for 5 minutes. This makes a thin syrup with fewer calories.

Unsweetened Fruit

Unsweetened berries can be canned in their own juice, in extracted juice or in water. Thus canned, berries will not spoil but may be less colorful and may lose some of their flavor. Process as for sweetened berries.

A wet towel, placed over a slanted board with a large container such as a plastic dishpan at the bottom, makes an excellent berry cleaner. It is especially good for firm fruits like cranberries and blueberries. Simply pour the berries onto the top of the incline slowly and allow them to roll down and into the container at the bottom. Most debris such as twigs, leaves and the like will stick to the damp towel. It doesn't get all the extraneous matter, however, but you won't need to do much more picking over.

FREEZING BERRIES

Berries must be in top condition for freezing well. Do not use underripe or overripe fruit or any that is beginning to spoil. This means picking over the berries carefully and discarding unsuitable fruit. Work rapidly when preparing berries for the freezer. Have all needed supplies gathered and ready before berries are prepared to ensure getting the fruit into the freezer without undue delay.

Containers for Berry Freezing

Used milk cartons and glass containers are not recommended for containing frozen berries. For dry pack, plastic freezer bags are good. The little sandwich bags are not strong enough, so be sure to use a sturdier bag. Flexible or rigid plastic containers with lids are excellent, particularly if the square ones are used which fit together well and waste little space in storage. Round containers can be used, but they waste freezer space.

Freezing in Quantity

Clean blueberries or lowbush cranberries and spread on cookie sheets or heavy duty foil trays. Be sure they are dry and do not cling together. Then place in freezer and freeze until they are hard. Empty into a fair-sized plastic bag and close it airtight. You can freeze a big bag full of these, and they will remain separated from each other. When you want a few just open the bag and take out the amount needed. Replace the bag in the freezer without thawing for use later on. This is the same way we now buy some fruits and vegetables in the market. Just be sure you don't leave the berries on the cookie sheets too long after they are frozen or they will become dehydrated. They need to be kept airtight.

Leave Some in the Freezer

Don't preserve all your frozen fruit. Leave some for use in breads, cookies, meat dishes and other goodies, during the winter. It is especially nice to have a few lowbush cranberries to dip into when you want to make a loaf of Cranberry Nut Bread. Any that are left over you can always make into jam or something else before the new crop comes on.

176 —

Freezing Out of Doors

Lowbush cranberries, blueberries and huckleberries may be stored out of doors to freeze if you live in the right climate for it. Clean berries and be sure there are no imperfect berries or berries that are overripe. If you have a mesh bag such as onions once were sold in, you are in luck. Otherwise improvise by using an old pillowcase or other cloth bag. It is essential that the berries get air circulation so don't use plastic or other such bags. Perhaps you could use several thicknesses of cheesecloth to make a bag. One thickness is not strong enough. Do not put more than a couple quarts of the berries in one bag. Hang them up out of doors (under the eaves of the house, perhaps) within easy reach. You don't want to wade through deep snow to reach them later on. The berries will stay in excellent condition as long as the weatherman provides freezing temperatures, a long time in some parts of Alaska!

Thawing Frozen Berries

Thaw berries in unopened containers at room temperature. All fruits tend to darken and lose flavor once they are thawed so use them as soon as possible after thawing.

Fruits meant for a frozen dessert are best left slightly frozen as cream or sauce hastens the thawing.

Berries to be used in pies or cobblers or similar dishes need to be defrosted only enough to separate the fruit.

No thawing is necessary if berries are to be cooked in sauces, jam, preserves and the like.

Tips for Freezing Berries

Dead ripe fruit that is too ripe for normal freezing can be made into a puree by crushing in a kettle. Add a small amount of water and bring to the boiling point. Cook slowly for 5 minutes. Press the berries through a sieve or strainer. Package in freezer containers with ½ cup sugar to each 4 cups of puree and freeze as soon as puree is completely cold.

Fruit juices may be frozen satisfactorily if you have ample room in your freezer. Simmer berries with just enough water to keep from sticking, for about 5 minutes. Extract the juice by pouring hot fruit into a wet jelly bag and allowing to drain for several hours or overnight. Do not squeeze bag as that will make the juice cloudy instead of clear. When juice is cold, package in freezer containers and freeze.

Skins of blueberries and huckleberries tend to toughen in freezing. That is why these berries should be scalded with steam or by placing berries in a colander and lowered into boiling water for 1 minute.

Always put containers of wild berries in the freezer as soon as prepared. Otherwise hold them in the refrigerator until you can put them in the freezer. Quick freezing is mandatory for berries.

Always leave a little head space in your freezer container — half an inch is enough.

Be sure to label and indicate date of freezing so that you can control your frozen berry inventory.

BERRY FREEZING CHART

Berries	Selection	Preparation	Safe Life of Berries in Freezer
Blueberries, all species	Firm, ripe berries	Wash in very cold water and scald in steam for one minute. Put in cold water to chill quickly. Dry pack.	18 months
Lowbush cranberries	Firm, ripe berries	Wash only if necessary. No sugar or syrup needed. Dry pack.	24 months
Red currants	Firm, good color	Wash only if needed and remove stems. One cup sugar to each three cups currants.	9 months
Other currants		Not recommended for freezing	
Raspberries	Firm, ripe, perfect	Do not wash unless absolutely necessary; handle carefully. Pack dry or with one cup sugar to four cups berries.	9 months

Berries	Selection	Preparation	Safe Life of Berries in Freezer
Salmonberries, cloudberries, nagoonberries, and similar berries		Handled the same as raspberries	9 months
Gooseberries	Firm, ripe, good color	Wash if needed. Crush slightly to stimulate juice. One cup sugar to three cups berries.	9 months
Strawberries	Firm, ripe, perfect	Prepare as soon after gathering as possible as strawberries lose their flavor rapidly. Hull but do not wash unless really needed. Pack dry or use ½ cup sugar to four cups of fruit.	9 months
Rose hips	Ripe, pick just before first frost	Clean and remove seeds with tip of knife. See recipe for Rose Hip Juice. Freezer containers instead of jars.	6 months
Highbush cranberries		Not recommended for freezing	
Huckleberries Crowberries Serviceberries Salal		Same as for blueberries	18 months 12 months 12 months 12 months
Oregon Crab Apple	Firm, ripe fruit	Make into puree or apple sauce	6 months

Most people go for drives in the summertime and the drive could well end at a good berry patch. Make it a point always to carry a pail or two and a few strong plastic bags in your car so that when you do happen on to a good patch you will have something to use for picking the berries.
Alaska Wild Berry Trails

—179

DRYING BERRIES

Drying wild berries is a particularly fruitful (sorry!) project for those who live in the bush or elsewhere far from supermarkets. It is reported that when dried, berries retain much of their nutritional value, too.

Checking Berries For Drying

Berries with thick or tough skins, such as blueberries, serviceberries and crowberries, should be checked before attempting to dry. Otherwise only the skin will dry and the inside of the berry will remain moist. Checking is accomplished by placing a small amount of the berries at a time in a colander (or cloth bag) and dunking in boiling water for one minute. Drain thoroughly as the berries should harbor no excess moisture before being spread to dry.

Basic Ways to Prepare Berries for Drying

There are two basic ways to dry our wild berries. They may be dried whole or they may be first made into a puree which can then be dried. Those that have small seeds respond well to the first method. Large seeded fruit, such as rose hips or highbush cranberries, are best seeded first or else dried by the puree method.

Drying Berries by Other Methods

It is possible to make your own dryer with several shelves for holding the berries as they dry. There are commercial dryers for home use on the market, too. However, unless you plan to go into drying in a big way, the sun- or oven-dried methods will do well enough. The sun-dried fruit seems to have the best flavor; probably that is natural.

Oven-Dried Berries

Whole berries may also be dried in the oven. Set oven at lowest heat. Line a cookie sheet with a single layer of paper towels and thinly spread out the berries. Put in the oven and leave the oven door ajar a bit. You may need to prop the door open with a pencil or other small stick. This is done to allow moisture to escape and to keep the berries drying slowly. They are to be dried and not cooked.

Puree Method of Drying Berries

Place berries in a saucepan with a small amount of water. If they are quite juicy no water will be required. Stir over low heat until the berries are soft. Put them through a sieve or food mill to obtain a smooth paste or puree. The puree is then spread thinly on sheets of waxed paper. They can be either dried out of doors in the sun or oven dried as with whole berries. When completely dry the puree may be broken into small chunks or chips and put in plastic bags to store in the freezer.

Rose Hip Powder

Rose hip powder may be made by crushing dried puree with a rolling pin until it is fine enough to suit you. This may be stored in small jars in a cool, dry place. It is good to sprinkle over cereal and to include in hot cakes and other dishes to give Vitamin C as needed. The dry rose hips lose some of their vitamin content, still they retain a lot, and, though adding little flavor to anything, they are useful for their vitamin content.

Storing Dried Berries

Dried berries should be stored in a cool dry place. They can be put up in plastic bags or stored in screw-top jars. It is a good idea to inspect dried fruit occasionally since sometimes they become a bit moldy. This is because they were not dried thoroughly enough.

Using Dried Berries

The whole dried berries may be used like raisins or commercially dried currants; or they may be reconstituted by adding a little water and allowing to soak for an hour or so, then simmering gently for a few minutes before using. The puree may be reconstituted in similar fashion. It can also be crushed with a rolling pin and added to puddings, pies and other berry dishes.

GLOSSARY

Alpine — Growing above timber line in mountain areas.

Annual — A plant whose term of life is limited to a single growing season.

Biennial — A plant whose normal life cycle stretches over two years, flowering and fruiting only during the second year.

Bloom — A powdery coating seen on some fruits and leaves.

Bract — A kind of leaf or leaflike shape most often located at the base of a flower.

Circumboreal — Surrounding the north; around the Northern Hemisphere.

Compound — Made up of two or more parts or sections.

Endemic — Native to a particular area, as with certain plant species.

Evergreen — Green throughout the entire year, the leaves of one season not dropping until the new leaves have grown.

Family — A major subdivision in the classification of plants.

Habit — The characteristic form or growth mode of a plant.

Habitat — The environment where a plant is normally found to grow.

Heath — An open area of land grown over with coarse plants.

Hip — Ripened fruit of the rose.

Hybridize — Produce a different species by crossing or mingling of two species.

Indigenous — Occurring naturally in place specified; native to the place.

Muskeg — Bog or marsh formed by many deposits of leaves, mosses, muck and the like.

Raceme — The arrangement of flowers on short stalks radiating from a common axis on a plant's stem or stems.

Range — The geographical area throughout which a plant exists.

Scurfy — Resembling, producing or covered with small scales or incrustations.

Species — The particular biological classification for related plants that resemble one another and that normally breed only among themselves.

Station — A place in which a particular species of plant may be found.

Subalpine — Of, pertaining to, or growing in mountain regions near, but below, timber line.

Timber line — The level on a mountainside above which timber will not grow.

Tundra — Rolling, treeless, sometimes marshy plain, usually found only in arctic or near-arctic regions.

Whorl — Set of leaves on same plane and distributed around a stem in a circle; radiating from one point.

Indexes

Three indexes to the berries of Alaska are provided to aid in identifying and cross referencing species. A fourth index is for the recipes. The Index by Family Names provides an alphabetical listing by the main family groupings into which berries are divided. Under each family name are given the botanical names and the common names.

The Index by Botanical Names provides a listing by the scientific names with the appropriate common names indicated. And finally, the Index by Common Names lists the most used common names with their relevant botanical names.

In many instances, common names for berries differ greatly in various parts of our land. For example, the Canadian dwarf dogwood is also called crackerberry, dwarf cornel, cornel, miniature dogwood, ground dogwood, dwarf dogwood, bunchberry and pudding berry, depending on where you live.

Blueberries probably enjoy more names than any other wild berry, no doubt because they are so widespread in their habitats. Some of these many names are: whortleberry, bilberry, dwarf bilberry, huckleberry, Sierra bilberry, great bilberry, bog bilberry, mountain bilberry, twin-leaved huckleberry, blue huckleberry, lowbush blueberry, swamp blueberry, farkleberry, Blueridge blueberry, box blueberry, big whortleberry, sour-top blueberry, velvet-leaf blueberry, early blueberry, Alaska blueberry, black huckleberry, deerberry, squaw huckleberry, tangleberry, sugar blueberry, western blueberry, thin-leaf blueberry, dangleberry and more.

We have not attempted to provide an exhaustive list of all common names; as we have just suggested, that would require a complete volume of its own. Where multiple names do exist, we have provided the three or four most frequently encountered.

CROWFOOT
  Actaea rubra — 10
    Baneberry
CYPRESS
  Juniperus communis — 2
    Juniper
    Common Juniper
    Mountain Juniper
DOGWOOD
  Cornus canadensis — 35
    Canadian Dwarf Dogwood
    Bunchberry
    Dwarf Cornel
    Miniature Dogwood
  Cornus stolonifera — 33
    Red-Osier Dogwood
    American Dogwood
    Red Stem Dogwood
  Cornus suecica — 34
    Swedish Cornel
    Lapland Cornel
GINSENG
  Echinopanax horridum — 32
    Devil's Club
  Oplopanax horridum — 32
    Devil's Club
GOOSEFOOT
  Chenopodium capitatum — 9
    Strawberry Blite
    Strawberry Spinach
    Squaw Paint
HEATH
  Arctostaphylos alpina — 39
    Bearberry
    Alpine Bearberry
    Ptarmigan Berry
  Arctostaphylos rubra — 39
    Bearberry
  Arctostaphylos uva-ursi — 38
    Kinnikinnick
    Bearberry
    Meal Berry
  Empetrum nigrum — 36
    Crowberry
    Mossberry
    Blackberry

Gaultheria miqueliana — 37
    Salal
Gaultheria shallon — 37
    Salal
Oxycoccus microcarpus — 45
    Bog Cranberry
    True Cranberry
    Swamp Cranberry
Vaccinium alaskensis
(V. alaskaense) — 43
    Alaska Blueberry
Vaccinium ovalifolium — 42
    Early Blueberry
    Blue Huckleberry
Vaccinium parvifolium — 41
    Red Huckleberry
Vaccinium uliginosum — 44
    Bog Blueberry
    Alpine Blueberry
    Bog Bilberry
Vaccinium vitis-idaea — 40
    Lowbush Cranberry
    Lingonberry
    Mountain Cranberry
HONEYSUCKLE
  Lonicera involucrata — 49
    Honeysuckle
    Black Twinberry
    Bearberry Honeysuckle
  Sambucus racemosa — 46
    Red Elderberry
    Pacific Red Elder
  Symphoricarpos albus — 48
    Snowberry
  Viburnum edule — 47
    Highbush Cranberry
LILY
  Clintonia uniflora — 3
    Blue Bead
    Single-flowered Clintonia
    Queen's Cup

Maianthemum dilatatum
(Unifolium dilatatum) — 51
   Deerberry
   False Lily-of-the-Valley
   Wild Lily-of-the-Valley
Smilacina racemosa — 4
Smilacina stellata — 4
   False Solomon's Seal
   Star-flowered Solomon's Seal
Streptopus amplexifolius — 6
   Twisted Stalk
   Watermelon Berry
   Cucumber Root
Streptopus roseus — 7
   Rosy Twisted Stalk
OLEASTER
Elaeagnus commutata — 31
   Silverberry
Shepherdia canadensis — 30
   Soapberry
   Soopalallie
ROSE
Amelanchier alnifolia — 19
   Serviceberry
   Shadbush
   Juneberry
Amelanchier florida — 19
   Pacific Serviceberry
   Juneberry
Fragaria chiloensis — 27
   Beach Strawberry
Fragaria virginiana — 25
   Wild Strawberry
Malus fusca — 17
   Oregon Crab Apple
   Western Crab Apple
Rosa acicularis — 29
   Prickly Wild Rose
   Wild Rose
Rosa nutkana — 29
   Nootka Rose
   Wild Rose
Rosa woodsii — 29
   Woods Rose
   Wild Rose
Rubus arcticus — 22
   Nagoonberry
   Wineberry

Rubus chamaemorus — 21
   Cloudberry
   Baked Apple Berry
   Salmonberry
Rubus idaeus — 23
   Raspberry
   Red Raspberry
Rubus leucodermis — 28
   Black Raspberry
   Black Cap
Rubus parviflorus — 26
   Thimbleberry
Rubus pedatus — 20
   Five-leaved Bramble
   Trailing Raspberry
Rubus spectabilis — 24
   Salmonberry
Rubus stellatus — 22
   Nagoonberry
   Wineberry
Sorbus scopulina — 18
   Western Mountain Ash
Sorbus sitchensis — 18
   Sitka Mountain Ash
SANDALWOOD
Geocaulon lividum — 8
   Northern Commandra
   Timberberry
SAXIFRAGE
Ribes bracteosum — 12
   Stink Currant
Ribes glandulosum — 14
   Skunk Currant
Ribes hudsonianum — 13
   Northern Black Currant
Ribes lacustre — 11
   Bristly Black Currant
   Swamp Gooseberry
Ribes laxiflorum — 15
   Trailing Black Currant
Ribes triste — 16
   Northern Red Currant
   American Red Currant

Actaea rubra — 10
  Baneberry
Amelanchier alnifolia — 19
  Serviceberry
  Shadbush
  Juneberry
Amelanchier florida — 19
  Pacific Serviceberry
  Juneberry
Arctostaphylos alpina — 39
  Bearberry
  Alpine Bearberry
  Ptarmigan Berry
Arctostaphylos rubra — 39
  Bearberry
Arctostaphylos uva-ursi — 38
  Kinnikinnick
  Bearberry
  Meal Berry
Chenopodium capitatum — 9
  Strawberry Blite
  Strawberry Spinach
  Squaw Paint
Clintonia uniflora — 3
  Blue Bead
  Single-flowered Clintonia
  Queen's Cup
Cornus canadensis — 35
  Canadian Dwarf Dogwood
  Bunchberry
  Dwarf Cornel
  Miniature Dogwood
Cornus stolonifera — 33
  Red-Osier Dogwood
  American Dogwood
  Red Stem Dogwood
Cornus suecica — 33
  Swedish Cornel
  Lapland Cornel
Echinopanax horridum — 32
  Devil's Club
Elaeagnus commutata — 31
  Silverberry
Empetrum nigrum — 36
  Crowberry
  Mossberry
  Blackberry

Fragaria chiloensis — 27
  Beach Strawberry
Fragaria virginiana — 25
  Wild Strawberry
Gaultheria miqueliana — 37
  Salal
Gaultheria shallon — 37
  Salal
Geocaulon lividum — 8
  Northern Commandra
  Timberberry
Juniperus communis — 2
  Juniper
  Common Juniper
  Mountain Juniper
Lonicera involucrata — 49
  Honeysuckle
  Black Twinberry
  Bearberry Honeysuckle
Maianthemum dilatatum — 5
  Deerberry
  False Lily-of-the-Valley
  Wild Lily-of-the-Valley
Malus fusca — 17
  Oregon Crab Apple
  Western Crab Apple
Oplopanax horridum — 32
  Devil's Club
Oxycoccus microcarpus — 45
  Bog Cranberry
  True Cranberry
  Swamp Cranberry
Ribes bracteosum — 12
  Stink Currant
Ribes glandulosum — 14
  Skunk Currant
Ribes hudsonianum — 13
  Northern Black Currant
Ribes lacustre — 11
  Bristly Black Currant
  Swamp Gooseberry
Ribes laxiflorum — 15
  Trailing Black Currant

INDEX BY BOTANICAL NAMES

Ribes triste — 16
    Northern Red Currant
    American Red Currant
Rosa acicularis — 29
    Wild Rose
    Prickly Wild Rose
Rosa nutkana — 29
    Wild Rose
    Nootka Rose
Rosa woodsii — 29
    Wild Rose
    Woods Rose
Rubus arcticus — 22
    Nagoonberry
    Wineberry
Rubus chamaemorus — 21
    Cloudberry
    Baked Apple Berry
    Salmonberry
Rubus idaeus — 23
    Raspberry
    Red Raspberry
Rubus leucodermis — 28
    Black Raspberry
    Black Cap
Rubus parviflorus — 26
    Thimbleberry
Rubus pedatus — 20
    Five-leaved Bramble
    Trailing Raspberry
Rubus spectabilis — 24
    Salmonberry
Rubus stellatus — 22
    Nagoonberry
    Wineberry
Sambucus racemosa — 46
    Red Elderberry
    Pacific Red Elder
Shepherdia canadensis — 30
    Soapberry
    Soopalallie
Smilacina racemosa — 4
    False Solomon's Seal
    Star-flowered Solomon's Seal

Smilacina stellata — 4
    False Solomon's Seal
Sorbus scopulina — 18
    Western Mountain Ash
Sorbus sitchensis — 18
    Sitka Mountain Ash
Streptopus amplexifolius — 6
    Twisted Stalk
    Watermelon Berry
    Cucumber Root
Streptopus roseus — 7
    Rosy Twisted Stalk
Symphoricarpus albus — 48
    Snowberry
Unifolium dilatatum — 5
    Deerberry
    False Lily-of-the-Valley
    Wild Lily-of-the-Valley
Vaccinium alaskaense — 43
    Alaska Blueberry
Vaccinium alaskensis — 43
    Alaska Blueberry
Vaccinium ovalifolium — 42
    Early Blueberry
    Blue Huckleberry
Vaccinium parvifolium — 43
    Red Huckleberry
Vaccinium uliginosum — 44
    Bog Blueberry
    Alpine Blueberry
    Bog Bilberry
Vaccinium vitis-idaea — 40
    Lowbush Cranberry
    Lingonberry
    Mountain Cranberry
Viburnam edule — 47
    Highbush Cranberry

Alaska Blueberry
  Vaccinium alaskaense — 43
  v. alaskensis — 43
Alpine Bearberry — 39
  Arctostaphylos alpina
Alpine Blueberry — 44
  Vaccinium uliginosum
American Dogwood — 33
  Cornus stolonifera
American Red Currant — 16
  Ribes triste
Baked Apple Berry — 21
  Rubus chamaemorus
Baneberry — 10
  Actaea rubra
Beach Strawberry — 27
  Fragaria chiloensis
Bearberry
  Arctostaphylos alpina — 39
  A. rubra — 39
  A. uva-ursi — 38
Bearberry Honeysuckle — 49
  Lonicera involucrata
Blackberry — 36
  Empetrum nigrum
Black Cap — 28
  Rubus leucodermis
Black Raspberry — 28
  Rubus leucodermis
Black Twinberry — 49
  Lonicera involucrata
Blue Bead — 3
  Clintonia uniflora
Blue Huckleberry — 42
  Vaccinium ovalifolium
Bog Bilberry — 44
  Vaccinium uliginosum
Bog Blueberry — 44
  Vaccinium uliginosum
Bog Cranberry — 45
  Oxycoccus microcarpus
Bristly Black Currant — 11
  Ribes lacustre

Bunchberry — 35
  Cornus canadensis
Canadian Dwarf Dogwood — 35
  Cornus canadensis
Cloudberry — 21
  Rubus chamaemorus
Common Juniper — 2
  Juniperus communis
Crowberry — 36
  Empetrum nigrum
Cucumber Root — 6
  Streptopus amplexifolius
Deerberry
  Maianthemum dilatatum — 5
  Unifolium dilatatum — 5
Devil's Club
  Echinopanax horridum — 32
  Oplopanax horridum — 32
Dwarf Cornel — 35
  Cornus canadensis
Early Blueberry — 42
  Vaccinium ovalifolium
False Lily-of-the-Valley
  Maianthemum dilatatum — 5
  Unifolium dilatatum — 5
False Solomon's Seal
  Smilacina racemosa — 4
  Smilacina stellata — 4
Five-leaved Bramble — 20
  Rubus pedatus
Highbush Cranberry — 47
  Viburnum edule
Honeysuckle — 49
  Lonicera involucrata
Juneberry
  Amelanchier alnifolia — 19
  Amelanchier florida — 19

Juniper — 2
Juniperus communis
Kinnikinnick — 38
Arctostaphylos uva-ursi
Lapland Cornel — 33
Cornus suecica
Lingonberry — 40
Vaccinium vitis-idaea
Lowbush Cranberry — 40
Vaccinium vitis-idaea
Meal Berry — 38
Arctostaphylos uva-ursi
Miniature Dogwood — 35
Cornus canadensis
Mossberry — 36
Empetrum nigrum
Mountain Cranberry — 40
Vaccinium vitis-idaea
Mountain Juniper — 2
Juniper communis
Nagoonberry
Rubus arcticus — 22
Rubus stellatus — 22
Nootka Rose — 29
Rosa nutkana
Northern Black Currant — 13
Ribes hudsonianum
Northern Commandra — 8
Geocaulon lividum
Northern Red Currant — 16
Ribes triste
Oregon Crab Apple — 17
Malus fusca
Pacific Red Elder — 46
Sambucus racemosa
Pacific Serviceberry — 19
Amelanchier florida
Prickly Wild Rose — 29
Rosa acicularis
Ptarmigan Berry — 39
Arctostaphylos alpina
Queen's Cup — 3
Clintonia uniflora

Raspberry — 23
Rubus idaeus
Red Elderberry — 46
Sambucus racemosa
Red Huckleberry — 43
Vaccinium parvifolium
Red-Osier Dogwood — 33
Cornus stolonifera
Red Raspberry — 23
Rubus idaeus
Red Stem Dogwood — 33
Cornus stolonifera
Rosy Twisted Stalk — 7
Streptopus roseus
Salal
Gaultheria miqueliana — 37
Gaultheria shallon — 37
Salmonberry
Rubus chamaemorus — 21
Rubus spectabilis — 24
Serviceberry — 19
Amelanchier alnifolia
Shadbush — 19
Amelanchier alnifolia
Silverberry — 31
Elaeagnus commutata
Single-flowered Clintonia — 3
Clintonia unifolia
Sitka Mountain Ash — 18
Sorbus sitchensis
Skunk Currant — 14
Ribes glandulosum
Snowberry — 48
Symphoricarpus albus
Soapberry — 30
Shepherdia canadensis
Soopalallie — 30
Shepherdia canadensis
Squaw Paint — 9
Chenopodium capitatum
Star-flowered Solomon's Seal — 4
Smilacina stellata

INDEX BY COMMON NAMES

Stink Currant — 12
  Ribes bracteosum
Strawberry Blite — 9
  Chenopodium capitatum
Strawberry Spinach — 9
  Chenopodium capitatum
Swamp Cranberry — 45
  Oxycoccus microcarpus
Swamp Gooseberry — 11
  Ribes lacustre
Swedish Cornel — 33
  Cornus suecica
Thimbleberry — 26
  Rubus parviflorus
Timberberry — 26
  Geocaulon lividum
Trailing Black Currant — 15
  Ribes laxiflorum
Trailing Raspberry — 20
  Rubus pedatus
True Cranberry — 45
  Oxycoccus microcarpus

Twisted Stalk — 6
  Streptopus amplexifolius
Watermelon Berry — 6
  Streptopus amplexifolius
Western Crab Apple — 17
  Malus fusca
Western Mountain Ash — 18
  Sorbus scopulina
Wild Lily-of-the-Valley
  Maianthemum dilatatum — 5
  Unifolium dilatatum — 5
Wild Rose
  Rosa acicularis — 29
  Rosa nutkana — 29
  Rosa woodsii — 29
Wild Strawberry — 25
  Fragaria virginiana
Wineberry
  Rubus arcticus — 22
  Rubus stellatus — 22
Woods Rose — 29
  Rosa Woodsii

Italicized entries show that a particular recipe from the book is used in making another.

Bar-B-Q Sauce, 81
Bars
    assorted berries in, 127
    lowbush cranberries in, 126
    strawberry preserves in, 128, 129
Basic Cranberry Nut Bread, 80
Berry(ies),
    assorted, in: bars, 127; dessert
        sauce, 139
    canned, in pancakes, 60
    canning, see Canning berries
    crushed, in: frozen dessert, 131;
        trail food, 157
    dried, in: candy, 154; cookies,
        126, 128; frosting, 122;
        mincemeat, 135; muffins, 57;
        specialty bread, 62
    drying, see Drying berries
    freezing, see Freezing berries
    jam in cookies, 124, 127, 128
    jelly in cookies, 124
    juice in: cookies, 124; dessert
        sauce, 137
    substitutions, 53
    Mixed, Syrup, 155
Biscuits
    blueberry, 56
    huckleberry, 56
    Whole Berry Cranberry Sauce in,
        56
Blackberries (see also Crowberries)
    in Eskimo ice cream, 158
Breads, see Specialty bread
Buns, 57
Butter
    highbush cranberry puree in, 165
    rose hip, 166-167
Blueberry(ies),
    Bannock, 59
    biscuits, 56
    Cake, 111
    candy, 152
    canned, in muffins, 57
    Cheesecake, 112
    chilled dessert, 129
    Cup Cakes, 119

dessert sauce, 138
dried, in: specialty bread, 61; trail
    food, 157
Eskimo ice cream, 158
frozen desserts, 134
in Northland Mincemeat, 136
Jelly, 161
juice in: dinner sauce, 137;
    mincemeat, 136
. pancakes, 59, 60
pies, 92, 94, 96
preserves, 165
puddings, 104, 105, 107
puree in candy, 152
salads, 68
Shortcake, 122
Sponge Cake, 112
sweet rolls, 66
Syrup, 154
tapioca, 110
tarts, 100
torte, 120
Upside Down Cake, 113
Wine, 147
Blueberry Syrup
    in dinner sauce, 84
    recipe for, 154
Cake (see also Cup-, Upside down
    and Coffee cakes)
    blueberries in, 111, 112
    crab apple pieces in, 113
    Crab Apple Sauce in, 114, 116
    lowbush cranberries in, 115
    Lowbush Cranberry Juice, in, 114
    raspberries in, 111, 116, 117
    strawberries in, 110, 111, 116
    salmonberry jam in, 117
    Whole Berry Cranberry Sauce in,
        117; Whole Berry Cranberry
        Sauce and Cranberry Cheese
        Frosting, 118
Candy
    blueberries in, 152
    blueberry puree in, 152
    dried berries in, 154
    dried serviceberries in, 152

Lowbush Cranberry Juice in, 153, 154
raspberries in, 152
rose hips in, 153
Canning berries
in general, 170-71
boiling water bath, 171-72
sugar syrup chart, 173
sweetening: with sugar, 173; without sugar, 173
unsweetened fruit, 173
Catsups
highbush cranberry, 86
lowbush cranberry, 87
rose hip, 87
Cheesecake, Blueberry, 112
Chilled desserts
blueberries in, 129
canned lowbush cranberries in, 131
raspberries in, 135
strawberries in, 133, 134, 135
thimbleberries in, 134
Chutney
lowbush cranberry, 88
Cloudberry
Jelly, 164
Pie, 92
pudding, 103
tarts, 99
Cobbler
berries (any kind) in, 102
blueberry, 103
huckleberry, 103
lowbush cranberry, 102
Coffee cake
berry jam in, 66
lingonberries in, 65
lowbush cranberries in, 64, 65
Conserves
Wild Strawberry-Pineapple, 168
Cookies
berry jam in, 127
berry jam *and* dried berries in, 128
berry jam *and* juice in, 124
dried: berries *and* rose hips in, 126; currants in, 125, 126; serviceberries in, 125; watermelon berries in, 125

Crab apple(s),
cake, 113
in dessert sauce, 137
Jelly, 161
Crab Apple Sauce
cake, 114, 116
in dinner sauce, 81; specialty bread, 62
Mousse, 130
recipe for, 137
specialty bread, 62
Cranberries, *see* Highbush cranberries *and* Lowbush cranberries
Cranberry Cheese Frosting
recipe for, 121
with cake, 118
Cranberry "Mincemeat"
recipe for, 135
tarts, 101
Cranberry Syrup
in dinner sauce, 84
recipe for, 155
Crowberry(ies)
dried, in trail food, 157
Pie, 94
pudding, 106
Syrup, 155
Crepes
raspberry, 61
strawberry, 61
Crust(s)
recipe for: crumb, 90; 8- or 9-inch double or 10-inch single, 90; 8- or 9-inch single, 90; Master Mix, 90
Cupcakes
Blueberry, 119
Currant, 119
Wild Rose Petal, 120
Currant(s)
Cup Cakes, 119
dried, in: cookies, 125, 126; specialty bread, 61; steamed pudding, 108
jelly, 164
mead, 148
red, in jam, 166
preserves, 165, 167, 168
Dessert sauce
berry juice in, 137

blueberries in, 138
crab apples in, 137
lowbush cranberries in, 138
raspberries in, 138, 139
raspberries and *Wild Currant Jelly*
in, 138
red huckleberries in, 136
salmonberries and *Wild Currant*
Jelly in, 138
strawberries in, 138, 139
Tutti Frutti (assorted berries), 139
Whole Berry Cranberry Sauce, 137
Dinner sauce
Bar-B-Q, 81
blueberries in, 137
Blueberry Syrup in, 84
Crab Apple Sauce in, 81
Cranberry Syrup in, 84
dried rose hips in, 83
lowbush cranberries in, 82, 83
Lowbush Cranberry Juice in, 81,
83
juniper berries in, 84
Dressing(s)
lowbush cranberries in, 70, 71
Lowbush Cranberry Jelly in, 70
raspberry puree in, 71
strawberries in, 71, 72
strawberry preserves in, 72
Whole Berry Cranberry Sauce in,
70
Wild Currant Jelly in, 71
Drying berries
basic preparation for, 182
checking berries, 182
methods: oven-dried, 182;
puree, 182; rose hip powder,
183; other, 182
storage, 183
Eskimo and Indian Dishes
akutaq, 158
ice cream, 158
tiyulik, 158
Filling
strawberry, 122
nagoonberry, 122
Frosting
dried berries in, 122
lowbush cranberry, 121
Lowbush Cranberry Sauce in, 121

Freezing berries
chart for, 178-79
containers for, 176
in quantity, 176
out of doors, 176
thawing, 177
tips for, 177
Frozen dessert
Crab Apple Sauce in, 130
berries (any kind) in, 130, 131,
134
lowbush cranberries in, 132
Lowbush Cranberry Sauce in, 130
raspberries in, 132
strawberries in, 131, 133, 135
Highbush cranberry
Catsup, 75, 86
Jelly, 162
puree in butter, 165
Highbush Cranberry Catsup
in (moose or caribou) meat loaf,
75
recipe for, 86
Indian dishes, *see* Eskimo and Indian
Dishes
Jam
Raspberry-Currant, 166
Salmonberry: in cake, 117; recipe
for, 167
Strawberry Citrus, 167
Jelly
Blueberry, 161
Cloudberry, 164
Crab Apple, 161
Highbush Cranberry, 162
lowbush cranberry, 162
mountain ash berry, 161, 163
nagoonberry, 164
pectin test for, 160
Red Huckleberry, 163
Rose Hip, 163
Salmonberry, 164
"sheet" test for, 160
Wild Currant, 164
Wineberry, 164
Juice(s)
in syrup, 155
Lowbush Cranberry, 142
Rose Hip, 142

Lingonberries, *see* Lowbush
  cranberries
Liqueur
  lowbush cranberry, 147
  Raspberry, 148
Lowbush cranberry(ies)
  bars, 126
  cake, 114, 115
  canned, in: chilled desserts, 131;
    pancakes, 60
  Catsup, 87
  chutney, 88
  cobbler, 102
  coffee cake, 64, 65
  dessert sauce, 138
  dinner sauce, 82, 83, 84
  dressing, 71
  frosting, 121
  frozen dessert, 132, 134
  jelly: in ham dish, 74; in moose
    dish, 76; recipe for, 162
  liqueur, 147
  Juice, 142
  Marmalade, 166
  meat dish, 75
  "mincemeat," 135
  muffins, 58
  pancakes, 59
  pies, 93, 98
  preserve, 165
  punches without alcohol, 143, 144
  relish, 85
  salads, 69
  shortcake, 123
  specialty bread, 62, 63
  syrup, 155
  tapioca, 110
  upside down cake, 118
  wine, 147
Lowbush Cranberry Juice
  Bar-B-Q Sauce, 81
  cake, 114
  candy, 154
  dinner sauce, 81
  in meat dishes: chicken, 75;
    ground game meat or beef, 74;
    pork or bear spareribs, 76
  in Northland Mincemeat, 136
  marinade, 78, 79

  punch without alcohol, 143
  recipe for, 142
  salad, 69
Lowbush Cranberry Sauce
  frosting, 121
  dinner sauce, 83
  in meat dish (moose or caribou),
    77
  recipe for, 83
  salad, 69, 70
Lowbush Cranberry Jelly
  coffee cake, 64
  dressing, 70
  recipe for, 162
Marinade
  for: broiled flank steak, 78; fruit,
    78; game, 78; moose, 79;
    spareribs, 79
  Lowbush Cranberry Juice in, 78,
    79
Marmalade, lowbush cranberry, 166
Mead, currant, 148
Meat dishes
  berry juice in, 78
  caribou, 75, 77
  chicken, 75
  currant jelly in, 76
  dried serviceberries in, 76
  ground beef, 74, 75
  ground game meat, 74
  ham, 74, 76
  Highbush Cranberry Catsup in, 75
  lowbush cranberries in, 75
  lowbush cranberry jelly in, 74, 76
  lowbush cranberry syrup in, 76
  Lowbush Cranberry Juice in, 74,
    75, 76
  Lowbush Cranberry Sauce in, 77
  moose, 75, 76, 77
  pork chops, 77
  pork or bear spareribs, 76
  raspberry juice and Rose Hip Juice
    in, 77
  spareribs, 76, 78
Milk shake
  nagoonberry, 142
  Raspberry, 142
  strawberry, 142

Muffins,
  blueberry, 57
  dried berry, 57
  lowbush cranberry, 58
Mincemeat
  blueberries in, 136
  lowbush cranberries in, 135
Mountain ash berry
  jelly, 161, 163
Nagoonberry
  filling, 122
  Hardtack, 157
  jelly: juice in, 164; recipe for, 164
  milk shake, 142
  Pie, 96
  relish, 85
Oregon crab apples, *see* Crab apples
Pancakes
  blueberry, 59, 60
  Blueberry Bannock, 59
  canned berry (any kind), 60
  huckleberry, 59
  lowbush cranberry, 59, 60
Parfaits, *see* Frozen *or* Chilled
  desserts
Pectin, testing for, 160
Pie(s)
  Basic Wild Berry, 91
  blueberry, 92, 94, 96
  Cloudberry, 92
  Crowberry, 93
  lowbush cranberry, 93, 98
  Nagoonberry, 96
  raspberry, 91, 96-7
  rose hip, 97
  Salmonberry Cream, 98
  strawberry, 91, 95, 98, 99
Preserves
  blueberry-currant-lowbush
    cranberry-raspberry-strawberry,
    165
  currant, 167, 168
  strawberry, 168
Pudding
  blueberry, 104, 105, 107
  cloudberry, 103
  crowberry, 106
  raspberry jelly, 107
  salmonberry, 103
  Whole Berry Cranberry Sauce in,
    107

Punches
  with alcohol using:
    Lowbush Cranberry Juice, 145,
      146; strawberries, 144, 146
  without alcohol using:
    huckleberries, 144; lowbush
      cranberries, 143, 144; lowbush
      cranberries, rose hips *and*
      raspberries, 143; *Lowbush
      Cranberry Juice,* 143;
      raspberries, 145; raspberry
      juice, 144; strawberries, 145
Raspberry(ies)
  cake, 111, 116, 117
  candy, 152
  chilled dessert, 135
  -Currant Jam, 166
  defrosted, in dessert sauce, 138,
    139
  dessert sauce, 138
  filling, 122
  frozen dessert, 132, 134
  jam in crepes, 61
  Liqueur, 148
  pies, 91, 96-7
  preserve, 165
  punch without alcohol, 143, 144,
    145
  puree in salads, 71
  Rice Pudding, 107
  salad, 71
  steamed pudding, 109
  Syrup, 156
  tapioca, 110
  tarts, 99
Relish
  lowbush cranberry, 85
  Northland Mincemeat in, 85
  rose hip puree in, 86
  Whole Berry Cranberry Sauce in,
    85
Rose hip(s)
  butter, 166-67
  Candied, 153
  Catsup, 87
  dried, in: cookies, 126; dinner
    sauce, 82; trail food, 157; pie,
    97
  Jelly, 163

Juice, 142
Pie, 97
punch without alcohol, 143
puree in relish, 86
Syrup, 156
vitamin C content of, 53
Wild, Wine, 149
Rose Hip Juice
in meat (pork chop) dish, 77
recipe for, 142
tarts, 101
Rose petals cupcakes, 120
Salad(s)
Blueberry Nut, 68
Blueberry, 68
Frozen Strawberry, 70
lowbush cranberry, 69
Lowbush Cranberry Juice,
strawberries and strawberry
juice in, 69
Lowbush Cranberry Sauce in, 69,
70
Whole Berry Cranberry Sauce in,
68
Salal
dried, in cookies, 125
Salmonberry(ies)
cake, 111
Cream Pie, 98
dessert sauce, 138
Eskimo ice cream, 158
Jam, 167
Jelly, 164
milk shake, 142
Shortcake, 123
pudding, 103
tarts, 99
Sauces, *see* Dessert *and* Dinner
sauces
Serviceberries
dried, in: candy, 152; cookies,
125; meat (ham) dish, 76;
specialty bread, 61; trail food,
157
"Sheet" test for jelly, 160
Shortcake
Blueberry, 122
lowbush cranberry, 123
Salmonberry, 123
Strawberry, 124

Soapberries, *see also* Soopalallie
berries
Soopalallie berries
Indian Ice Cream, 158
Specialty bread
blueberries in, 61
Crab Apple Sauce in, 62
currants in, 61
lowbush cranberries in, 62, 63
serviceberries in, 61
Steamed pudding
dried currants and *Wild Currant
Jelly* in, 108
lowbush cranberry, 109
red huckleberry, 108
raspberry, 109
Strawberry(ies)
Baked Alaska, 133
cake, 110, 111, 116
chilled dessert, 134, 135
conserves, 168
dessert sauce, 138, 139
dressing, 72
filling, 122
frozen dessert, 131, 132
Ice Cream, 133
jam in: biscuits, 56; crepes, 61
jam, recipe for, 167
juice in salad, 69
milk shake, 142
Mousse, 133
pie, 91, 95, 98
preserves, recipes for, 165, 168
preserves in: bars, 128; cookies,
129; dressing, 72
salad, 69, 71
punch: with alcohol, 145; without
alcohol, 145
Shortcake, 124
tarts, 99, 100
Stuffing
Basic Cranberry Nut Bread in, 80
lowbush cranberries in, 80
Whole Berry Cranberry Sauce in,
79
Substituting berries, 53
Sweet Rolls
berry jam or jelly (any kind) in, 65
blueberries in, 66

Syrup
    berries and/or juice (any kind) in,
        155
    Blueberry, 154
    Crowberry, 155
    lowbush cranberry, 155
    Raspberry, 156
    Red Huckleberry, 156
    Rose Hip, 156
Tapioca
    lowbush cranberry, 110
    Old-Fashioned Blueberry, 110
    Raspberry, 110
Tarts
    blueberry, 100
    cloudberry, 99
    Cranberry "Mincemeat" in, 101
    raspberry, 99
    Rose Hip Juice and strawberry,
        101
    salmonberry, 99
    strawberry, 99, 100
Thimbleberries in chilled dessert, 134
Thimbleberry Whip (chilled dessert),
    134

Torte
    Blueberry Breakfast, 120
    lowbush cranberry, 121
Upside down cake
    Blueberry, 113
    lowbush cranberry, 118
Vitamin C, 53
Watermelon berries
    dried, in cookies, 125
Whole Berry Cranberry Sauce
    in: biscuits, 56; cake, 117, 118;
        dressing, 70; dessert sauce,
        137; pudding, 107; relish, 85;
        salad, 68; stuffing, 79;
    recipe for, 84
Wineberries, see Nagoonberries
Wines
    Blueberry, 147
    lowbush cranberry, 147
    Wild Rose Hip, 149
Wild Currant Jelly
    in: dessert sauce, 138;
        dinner sauce, 82; salad, 71;
        steamed pudding, 108
    recipe for, 164